Test Book

Multiple-choice Tests
Short-answer Tests

Great Source Education Group
a Houghton Mifflin Company
Wilmington, Massachusetts

www.greatsource.com

AUTHORS

Jim Burke
Author

Burlingame High School, Burlingame, California
Jim Burke, author of *Reading Reminders: Tools, Tips, and Techniques* and *The English Teacher's Companion,* has taught high school English for 13 years. His most recent books, *Tools for Thought* and *Illuminating Texts: How to Teach Students to Read the World,* further explore reading and those strategies that can help all students succeed in high school. He was the recipient of the California Reading Association's Hall of Fame Award in 2001 and the Conference on English Leadership's Exemplary English Leadership Award in 2000. He currently serves on the National Board of Professional Teaching Standards for English Language Arts.

Ron Klemp
Contributing Author

Los Angeles Unified School District, Los Angeles, California
Ron Klemp is the Coordinator of Reading for the Los Angeles Unified School District. He has taught Reading, English, and Social Studies and was a middle school Dean of Discipline. He is also a coordinator/facilitator at the Secondary Practitioner Center, a professional development program in the Los Angeles Unified School District. He has been teaching at California State University, Cal Lutheran University, and National University.

Wendell Schwartz
Contributing Author

Adlai Stevenson High School, Lincolnshire, Illinois
Wendell Schwartz has been a teacher of English for 36 years. For the last 24 years he also has served as the Director of Communication Arts at Adlai Stevenson High School. He has taught gifted middle school students for the last 12 years, as well as teaching graduate-level courses for National Louis University in Evanston, Illinois.

Editorial:
Design:
Illustrations:

Developed by Nieman, Inc. with Phil LaLeike
Ronan Design: Christine Ronan, Sean O'Neill, Maria Mariottini, Victoria Mullins
Mike McConnell

Printed in the United States of America

International Standard Book Number: 0-669-50420-3

1 2 3 4 5 6 7 8 9—MZ—08 07 06 05 04 03

Table of Contents

Introduction to Test Book

The *Test Book* includes short-answer tests and multiple-choice tests for each lesson in the *Reader's Handbook*. The test questions are based on the Quick Assess checklists found in the *Teacher's Guide*.

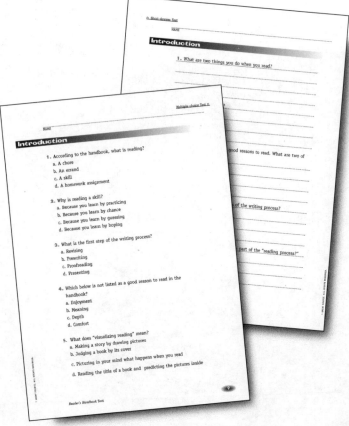

Use the tests as formal tools to assess students' understanding of the reading strategies and tools presented in the handbook.

Additional Assessment Tools

The *Reader's Handbook* program contains additional assessment tools in two other components:

Teacher's Guide

Each lesson in the *Teacher's Guide* ends with a page showing how to evaluate students' understanding of the lesson. Use the Quick Assess checklist to determine whether students should apply the strategies either a) independently or b) in guided practice in the *Student Applications Books*.

Lesson Plan Books

The *Lesson Plan Books* contain daily lessons for a 36-week school year. Each lesson ends with questions to use to assess students' understanding of the lesson.

NAME

Introduction

1. What are three reasons to read?

2. How are reading and writing both processes?

3. What is one characteristic of effective reading? Explain it.

4. How are the writing process and the reading process similar?

5. How has technology changed what and how we read?

NAME ....

Introduction

1. According to the *Reader's Handbook,* what is true of reading?

   a. It is boring.

   b. It requires tools.

   c. It does not require thought.

   d. It is not a process.

2. What is a characteristic of ineffective reading?

   a. Reading at home

   b. Reading at work

   c. Reading without making connections

   d. Reading in a quiet environment

3. The prewriting stage of the writing process is similar to which stage of the reading process?

   a. Prereading

   b. Revising

   c. Remembering

   d. Reading

4. How has technology changed what we read?

   a. Reading tastes have become similar.

   b. Reading occurs on devices, such as cell phones and computers.

   c. Reading has become outdated.

   d. Reading is limited to those who are writers and students.

5. Which of the following describes effective reading?

   a. Establishing a purpose for reading

   b. Checking your understanding as you read

   c. Reading with all of your senses

   d. All of the above

NAME ....

The Reading Process

1. What are the three main stages of the reading process?

....

....

....

2. How do you preview a reading?

....

....

....

3. What questions can you ask to connect to reading?

....

....

....

4. Why is rereading important?

....

....

....

5. How can good readers improve their ability to remember information?

....

....

....

NAME

The Reading Process

1. Which item below is NOT a step of the reading process?

a. Plan

b. Preview

c. Draft

d. Connect

2. Which is a characteristic of previewing?

a. Reading the supporting details

b. Browsing the index

c. Planning a reading strategy

d. Quickly skimming the material

3. Comparing a reading to your own life is doing which of the following?

a. Connecting

b. Previewing

c. Setting a Purpose

d. Rereading

4. What is true of rereading?

a. Rereading clarifies confusing parts of the reading.

b. Rereading always requires a new reading purpose.

c. Rereading involves memorizing key passages.

d. Rereading is part of the previewing step.

5. How can you remember the material you have read?

a. Read the material only once.

b. Read in a noisy environment.

c. Personalize the material and make it your own.

d. Reread all of the material word for word.

NAME ....

Reading Know-how

1. What do you do when you make an inference?

2. What do you do as you react and connect to the reading?

3. How do you find the implied main idea of a paragraph?

4. What are the characteristics of an expository paragraph?

5. How do you organize paragraphs in geographic order?

NAME ....

Reading Know-how

1. Making a value judgment is part of which of the following processes?

    a. Comparing and contrasting

    b. Making inferences

    c. Drawing conclusions

    d. Evaluating

2. Which method of reading actively includes listening to your own emotions?

    a. Highlighting

    b. Visualizing

    c. Reacting and connecting

    d. Clarifying

3. What is true of an implied main idea?

    a. It is stated clearly.

    b. It comes at the end of the selection.

    c. It must be inferred.

    d. It is controversial.

4. What is the purpose of a narrative paragraph?

    a. To tell a story

    b. To offer information

    c. To persuade

    d. To describe

5. What is the characteristic of classification order?

    a. Details are arranged to show similarities.

    b. Details are placed into categories or groups.

    c. Details are arranged in time order.

    d. Details are arranged by order of importance.

NAME ....

Reading History

1. What are three things to look for when previewing a history textbook?

   ....

   ....

   ....

2. Can you describe two note-taking tools useful for reading history?

   ....

   ....

   ....

3. What are two ways history textbooks are often organized? Explain each method.

   ....

   ....

   ....

4. Why is rereading a necessary step?

   ....

   ....

   ....

5. What is a good strategy to use for rereading, and why is it useful?

   ....

   ....

   ....

NAME

Reading History

1. What should you look for when previewing a history textbook?
    a. Index
    b. Headings
    c. Copyright information
    d. Glossary

2. Which of the following is a characteristic of Key Word or Topic Notes?
    a. They focus on the 5 W's and H questions.
    b. They are divided into two columns.
    c. They must be written in complete sentences.
    d. They are used as a preview activity.

3. What is one way history textbooks are often organized?
    a. Anecdotal order
    b. Comparison-contrast order
    c. Mixed order
    d. Geographic order

4. What is one way to set a purpose for reading history?
    a. Ask the questions *who, what, when, where, why,* and *how.*
    b. Study the last paragraph.
    c. Preview any photos or pictures.
    d. Reread everything.

5. Why is note-taking a useful strategy for reading history?
    a. It emphasizes classification.
    b. It helps readers remember plot events.
    c. It allows you to preview quickly.
    d. It helps you read actively and stay focused.

NAME

Reading Science

1. What are three things to look for when previewing a science chapter?

2. What is a good reading strategy to use when reading a science textbook? Describe.

3. Why is rereading important when reading a science textbook?

4. What is a good reading tool to use when reading a science textbook?

5. What are three common ways of organizing science writing?

NAME ....

Reading Science

1. What is one thing to look for when previewing a science chapter?
   a. Photos and their captions
   b. Descriptions of natural processes
   c. Detailed descriptions of animal life
   d. Author's name

2. Which of the following is a good reading strategy when reading a science textbook?
   a. Outlining
   b. Questioning the author
   c. Skimming
   d. Revising

3. What is a good way to set a purpose when reading science?
   a. Turn the title into a question.
   b. Review a list of objectives or goals.
   c. Base your purpose on a subheading or key terms.
   d. All of the above

4. Which of the following is a good tool to use with science textbooks?
   a. Argument Chart
   b. Plot Diagram
   c. Inference Chart
   d. Cause-Effect Organizer

5. Can you pick out the method below that is NOT a common way to organize science writing?
   a. Cause and effect
   b. Comparison and contrast
   c. Classification
   d. Problem and solution

NAME

Reading Math

1. What are three things to look for when previewing a math text?

2. How does visualizing and thinking aloud help you understand math problems?

3. How would you describe the organization of most math textbooks?

4. Why is rereading useful when using a math textbook?

5. What rereading strategy can you use to help you remember what you learned in a math chapter?

NAME

Reading Math

1. What should you look for when previewing a math text?

   a. The author's name

   b. Any answers to sample problems

   c. The date of publication

   d. Any listed goals

2. What is a useful strategy for reading math textbooks?

   a. Summarizing

   b. Paraphrasing

   c. Predicting

   d. Visualizing and thinking aloud

3. Which element normally ends a math chapter?

   a. Graphs

   b. Practice exercises

   c. Maps

   d. Opening explanation

4. Why should you reread portions of math textbooks?

   a. To fully comprehend the material

   b. To make personal connections to math problems

   c. To create your own math problems

   d. To draw graphs

5. How can you best help yourself remember what you learned?

   a. Read the first section of the math chapter again.

   b. Create practice tests.

   c. Redo easy homework problems.

   d. Read the first sentence of each paragraph.

NAME

Focus on Foreign Language

1. What types of information can be found in a foreign language textbook?

2. Why is note-taking important when studying a foreign language?

3. What is a good reading tool to use when reading a foreign language textbook?

4. How would you define *idiom*?

5. How can you review a foreign language chapter for a test?

NAME ....

Focus on Foreign Language

1. What type of material can often be found in a foreign language textbook?
   a. Speaking and writing assignments
   b. Grammar rules
   c. New vocabulary
   d. All of the above

2. Note-taking when reading a foreign language textbook helps you do which of the following?
   a. Understand the graphics
   b. Memorize new vocabulary
   c. Write essays
   d. Read faster

3. What is a good reading tool or strategy to use when reading a foreign language textbook?
   a. Web
   b. Storyboard
   c. Visualizing
   d. Paraphrase Chart

4. Which of the following is true of idioms in a foreign language?
   a. They are irregular verbs.
   b. They may be hard to remember.
   c. They are always made up of a single word.
   d. All of the above.

5. Why should you look at your notes after reading a chapter?
   a. To set a purpose
   b. To preview key vocabulary
   c. To plan a reading strategy
   d. To be sure they are clear and make sense

NAME

Focus on Science Concepts

1. What are three things to look for when previewing a science text?

2. Which two things do many science concepts involve?

3. How does a Flow Chart help you understand science concepts?

4. What are two ways to review the important information in a science reading?

5. How would you describe a science concept? Give an example of one.

NAME

Focus on Science Concepts

1. What is NOT something to look for when previewing a science text?

   a. Technical explanations

   b. Photos and captions

   c. Objectives

   d. Bulleted lists

2. Science concepts often include a description of which of these?

   a. Line graphs

   b. Processes

   c. Oral histories

   d. Photographs

3. Which is a good tip for making an Outline?

   a. Use the index to identify main topics.

   b. Don't start the Outline until you've finished reading.

   c. Don't try to write everything down.

   d. All of the above

4. What can you use a Flow Chart to show?

   a. Processes or a sequence of steps

   b. Key terms

   c. Photograph captions

   d. Headings

5. Which of the following best describes a science concept?

   a. A symbol

   b. A detailed history

   c. An illustration

   d. A general idea

NAME ....

Focus on Study Questions

1. What are the steps of the four-step plan for study questions?

2. How would you describe a good strategy for reading study questions?

3. What does *evaluate* mean in study questions?

4. Why does marking up a question help you answer it?

5. How can you help yourself find an answer to a difficult study question?

NAME

Focus on Study Questions

1. What is the first step of the four-step plan for study questions?
   a. Plan
   b. Write
   c. Reread
   d. Read

2. What is a good strategy for reading study questions?
   a. Questioning the author
   b. Reading critically
   c. Outlining
   d. Visualizing and thinking aloud

3. Which of the following terms means to "break down something into parts to examine its nature"?
   a. Hypothesize
   b. Interpret
   c. Analyze
   d. Predict

4. What does marking up a question emphasize?
   a. Adjectives
   b. Key words
   c. Nouns
   d. Words describing location

5. In a study question, what does *determine* mean?
   a. Find out exactly
   b. Calculate approximately
   c. Name
   d. Tell what something looks like

NAME

Focus on Word Problems

1. What is the four-step plan for solving a word problem?

2. Which reading strategy can you use when solving a word problem?

3. What does solving the problem in another way mean?

4. Why is estimating with simpler numbers a good method for checking your work?

5. How is working with a partner helpful for solving word problems?

NAME

Focus on Word Problems

1. What is the last step in the four-step plan for word problems?

a. Read

b. Check

c. Solve

d. Plan

2. Which reading tool or strategy should you use when solving a word problem?

a. Web

b. Double-entry Journal

c. Skimming

d. Visualizing and thinking aloud

3. Why is solving the problem in a different way useful?

a. It gives a different correct answer.

b. It paraphrases the word problem.

c. It helps you check the problem.

d. It takes less time.

4. What is the method of rounding off numbers to check a word problem called?

a. Estimating with simpler numbers

b. Guessing numbers

c. Working backward

d. Previewing numbers

5. Working with a partner involves doing which of the following things?

a. Debating

b. Copying

c. Reading aloud

d. Sharing ideas

NAME

Elements of Textbooks

1. What is a chapter preview?

2. How can you explain the difference between a chart and a graph?

3. How would you describe a footnote?

4. How are glossaries organized?

5. How would you define typography?

NAME ....

Elements of Textbooks

1. What is the purpose of a chapter preview?

    a. To summarize the ending of a chapter

    b. To give an idea of what will be read

    c. To focus on only one portion of the chapter

    d. To explain footnotes

2. Which of the following is NOT the purpose of a chart?

    a. To give information

    b. To show processes

    c. To be colorful

    d. To make comparisons

3. What is an alphabetical listing of a book's contents called?

    a. Sidebar

    b. Footnote

    c. Chart

    d. Index

4. What does a map legend explain?

    a. Why the map was made

    b. What the symbols on the map mean

    c. How to use the scale

    d. When the map was made

5. A timeline shows _____.

    a. a lot of random dots

    b. the answers to test questions

    c. the main ideas

    d. a sequence of events

NAME ....

Reading a Personal Essay

1. What are two purpose-setting questions that will help you read a

    personal essay?

    ....

    ....

    ....

2. How do you preview an essay?

    ....

    ....

    ....

3. What is a useful strategy for reading a personal essay?

    ....

    ....

    ....

4. In which pattern are most personal essays organized? Explain.

    ....

    ....

    ....

5. Why might you decide to reread a personal essay and what would be

    a good strategy to use?

    ....

    ....

    ....

NAME ....

Reading a Personal Essay

1. What are two common classifications of personal essays?
   a. Major and minor
   b. Formal and serious
   c. Dates and times
   d. Formal and informal

2. What is something to look for when previewing a personal essay?
   a. Graphic organizers
   b. Repeated words or phrases
   c. Journal entries
   d. Table of contents

3. Which of the following is a useful reading strategy for understanding the organization of a personal essay?
   a. Outlining
   b. Looking for cause and effect
   c. Skimming
   d. Paraphrasing

4. In which pattern are most personal essays organized?
   a. A circle
   b. A square
   c. A funnel
   d. A pyramid

5. What is a useful tool for identifying the supporting details and central point of personal essays?
   a. Argument Chart
   b. Main Idea Organizer
   c. Fiction Organizer
   d. Flow Chart

NAME

Reading an Editorial

1. How do you identify the author's viewpoint in an editorial?

2. How do you describe the strategy of questioning the author?

3. What does a Critical Reading Chart help you do?

4. What is a good tool for reading an editorial?

5. How is an editorial usually organized?

Reading an Editorial

1. What is an editorial?

   a. A humorous memoir

   b. A kind of persuasive writing

   c. A type of headline

   d. None of the above

2. Which of these should you use to set a purpose for reading an editorial?

   a. The date

   b. The headline

   c. The last body paragraph

   d. The last sentence

3. Which tool helps you evaluate information?

   a. Critical Reading Chart

   b. Story String

   c. Web

   d. Paraphrase Chart

4. Which strategy helps you pull together all the assertions and supporting details as you reread an editorial?

   a. Visualizing and thinking aloud

   b. Synthesizing

   c. Skimming

   d. Paraphrasing

5. Often a writer begins an editorial with which of the following items?

   a. Supporting details

   b. Recommendation

   c. Conclusion

   d. Assertion

NAME

Reading a News Story

1. Where are you likely to find information on the 5 W's and H in a

   news story?

2. How do you read critically?

3. Which reading tool can you use to help you read critically?

4. When might it make sense to reread a news story?

5. How is a typical news story organized?

NAME

Reading a News Story

1. What is true about a news story's lead?

   a. It's part of the headline.

   b. It's often the last paragraph.

   c. It is often at the beginning.

   d. It is always only one paragraph long.

2. What is the most important part of reading critically?

   a. Summarizing ideas in order

   b. Skimming the lead

   c. Asking yourself questions

   d. Assuming

3. Which reading tool helps you focus on whether there is another side of the story?

   a. Critical Reading Chart

   b. Outline

   c. Cause-Effect Organizer

   d. 5 W's and H Organizer

4. What is a good strategy to help you retell the most important ideas in a news story?

   a. Using graphic organizers

   b. Outlining

   c. Skimming

   d. Summarizing

5. In which shape is a typical news story organized?

   a. Square

   b. Inverted pyramid

   c. Inverted diamond

   d. Circle

NAME

Reading a Biography

1. How is a biography different from a piece of fiction?

2. What are two major goals of a biographer?

3. What are Sequence Notes?

4. How are most biographies organized?

5. What is a good rereading strategy to use with a biography? Describe it.

NAME

Reading a Biography

1. Which of these definitions describes a biographical subject?
   a. The person the biography is about
   b. A kind of personal letter
   c. A kind of diary
   d. The writer of the biography

2. Which of the following is a good tool to use when you want to make some conclusions about the influence of the events on a person?
   a. Venn Diagram
   b. Storyboard
   c. Inference Chart
   d. Classification Notes

3. Which reading tool helps you keep track of important events?
   a. Sequence Notes
   b. Character Map
   c. Nonfiction Organizer
   d. Setting Chart

4. How are most biographies organized?
   a. Geographic order
   b. Most to least important
   c. Chronological order
   d. Cause-effect Order

5. What are two good strategies to use with a biography?
   a. Summarizing and paraphrasing
   b. Looking for cause and effect and outlining
   c. Visualizing and thinking aloud and outlining
   d. Synthesizing and paraphrasing

NAME

Reading a Memoir

1. How is a memoir different from a novel?

2. What are three possible topics a memoir could cover?

3. What are Key Word or Topic Notes?

4. What are the two most common goals of a writer of a memoir?

5. What is synthesizing, and why is it a useful strategy for reading memoirs?

NAME

Reading a Memoir

1. What is a memoir?

a. A detailed story

b. A type of biographical writing

c. An editorial

d. A type of autobiographical writing

2. Which of the following is a topic generally covered by memoirs?

a. Major current events

b. Global problems

c. Actions of people the writer knew

d. General summaries of certain concepts

3. What do Key Word or Topic Notes help you remember?

a. Main ideas

b. Concluding sentences

c. Motifs

d. Symbols

4. What is a common feature of most memoirs?

a. They are short.

b. They are written in the first person.

c. They are written in the third person.

d. They deal with current events.

5. What items should you look for when you preview a memoir?

a. The title of each chapter

b. Any photographs or illustrations

c. Any summaries, quotations, or reviews

d. All of the above

NAME ....

Focus on Persuasive Writing

1. What are three things that persuasive writing may ask you to do?

....

....

....

2. In what way is the three-step plan for reading a persuasive piece of

writing useful?

....

....

....

3. Why is reading critically an important strategy for reading persuasive

writing?

....

....

....

4. How would you define *assertion*?

....

....

....

5. What are three examples of common propaganda techniques?

....

....

....

NAME

Focus on Persuasive Writing

1. Which of the following is an example of persuasive writing?
   a. Radio commercials
   b. Television advertising
   c. Election campaign posters
   d. All of the above

2. How do you take the first step in the three-step plan for focusing on persuasive writing?
   a. Decide what you think about the writer's argument.
   b. Find the supporting details.
   c. Find the conclusion.
   d. Find the topic.

3. Which is NOT one of the three parts of good persuasive writing?
   a. An assertion
   b. Support for the assertion
   c. Loaded words
   d. Acknowledgement of opposing viewpoints

4. What is an assertion?
   a. A statement of belief that the author explains and supports
   b. A conclusion that sums up the essay
   c. A good introduction
   d. A propaganda technique

5. Which propaganda technique involves changing the subject to distract someone from the real argument?
   a. Red herring
   b. Bandwagon appeal
   c. Straw man
   d. Broad generalization

NAME

Focus on Speeches

1. How can you differentiate between the two most common types of speeches?

2. When you look for the context of a speech as you preview, what are you trying to find?

3. What are the three parts of a speech?

4. What are name three common types of support for a viewpoint?

5. What are three common stylistic devices found in speeches?

Focus on Speeches

1. Which of the following is a common type of speech?

   a. Informative

   b. Descriptive

   c. First-person point of view

   d. Editorial

2. What is the last step of the four-step plan for focusing on a speech?

   a. Find the purpose.

   b. Find the main idea.

   c. Understand the organization.

   d. Evaluate the speech.

3. Which of the following is NOT one of the three standard parts of a speech?

   a. Introduction

   b. Body

   c. Chorus

   d. Conclusion

4. Which of the following is a type of support commonly used in good speeches?

   a. Broad generalizations

   b. Opinions of experts

   c. Prejudiced views

   d. Biased information

5. What does parallelism do for a speech?

   a. It makes it more confusing.

   b. It clarifies the topic.

   c. It adds rhythm to the speech.

   d. It distracts listeners.

© GREAT SOURCE. ALL RIGHTS RESERVED.

Reader's Handbook Test Book   **43**

NAME

Elements of Nonfiction

1. What is an assertion?

2. How are deductive and inductive reasoning different?

3. What does *denotation* mean?

4. What is a rhetorical question, and what is an example of a rhetorical question?

5. What is the usual purpose of satire?

Elements of Nonfiction

1. What is the purpose of an assertion?

   a. To confuse the reader

   b. To anger the reader

   c. To quote evidence

   d. To express a viewpoint

2. Which of the following is most associated with deductive reasoning?

   a. Specific to general

   b. General to specific

   c. Circular reasoning

   d. Descriptive writing

3. What kind of information does the lead of a news story contain?

   a. Opposing viewpoints

   b. A conclusion

   c. Answers to the 5 W's and H questions

   d. The author's bias

4. Which is jargon?

   a. Specialized or technical vocabulary

   b. A kind of irony

   c. An unsupported assertion

   d. A strong connotation

5. What do writers do when they use understatement?

   a. Exaggerate

   b. Intentionally say less than is complete or true

   c. Use lots of figurative language

   d. Use lots of irony

NAME

Reading a Short Story

1. What does it mean to synthesize?

2. Why is a Fiction Organizer effective for reading short stories?

3. What are the five parts of most short story plots?

4. How can you connect short stories to your own life?

5. Why is close reading a good rereading strategy?

NAME

Reading a Short Story

1. Synthesizing is a good strategy for doing which of the following?
   a. Creating descriptions
   b. Making inferences
   c. Considering several story elements at the same time
   d. Classifying the setting

2. What is true about a Cause-Effect Organizer?
   a. It focuses on literary symbols.
   b. It shows the reason something happens.
   c. It clarifies connotations.
   d. It gathers details on point of view.

3. What is the final part of most short story plots?
   a. Climax
   b. Exposition
   c. Falling action
   d. Resolution

4. What happens in the rising action part of a plot?
   a. The tension reaches a peak.
   b. Characters face a problem or conflict.
   c. Background information is established.
   d. The central problem is finally solved.

5. Which rereading strategy should you choose to look at part of a story in greater detail?
   a. Close reading
   b. Reading critically
   c. Outlining
   d. Skimming

NAME ....

Reading a Novel

1. What are four elements of a novel?

   ....

   ....

   ....

2. What are two tools useful for reading novels?

   ....

   ....

   ....

3. Why is the theme of a novel important?

   ....

   ....

   ....

4. What are three possible components of an author's style?

   ....

   ....

   ....

5. Why is it important to have a good reading strategy for novels?

   ....

   ....

   ....

NAME

Reading a Novel

1. What does point of view describe?

a. The cast of characters

b. The perspective from which an author tells a story

c. The narrator's education

d. The setting

2. What are two types of settings?

a. Old and new

b. Remote and near

c. General and immediate

d. Plain and detailed

3. What information is included on a Character Map?

a. What the character says and does

b. How a character looks and feels

c. What you feel about a character

d. All of the above

4. Why is using graphic organizers a good strategy to use with novels?

a. It is easy.

b. It avoids bias.

c. It let you skip previewing.

d. It gives you lots of ways to organize information.

5. Which of the following activities pulls together different parts of a novel and shows you how they fit together?

a. Inferring

b. Synthesizing

c. Making educated guesses

d. Paraphrasing

NAME ....

Focus on Plot

1. What are the five parts of the classic plot structure? ....

....

....

....

2. The beginning of most fiction pieces will tell you which three pieces ....

of information? ....

....

....

....

3. How would you define *flashback*? ....

....

....

....

4. How would you define *subplot*? ....

....

....

....

5. How does the plot of a story or novel relate to the theme? ....

....

....

....

Focus on Plot

1. Which of the following is part of the classic plot structure?

a. Analysis

b. Resolution

c. Dialogue

d. Thesis

2. Which of the following is true when you make a Plot Diagram?

a. You sketch what happens in the plot's climax.

b. You compare two stories.

c. You explain how plot affects theme.

d. You label the five parts of a plot.

3. What is a flashback?

a. A reference to the future

b. Commentary on current events

c. A reference to the past

d. A complaint

4. What is a subplot?

a. A smaller story within a story

b. A conflict

c. A minor theme

d. A setting within a setting

5. The exposition of a plot usually gives details about which of the following?

a. Symbols

b. Setting

c. Flashbacks

d. Subplots

NAME

Focus on Setting

1. Where are clues to the setting usually found?

2. What is an immediate setting?

3. What is mood, and how does setting create mood?

4. Why is close reading a good strategy for understanding the significance of setting?

5. Why is sketching the setting a good strategy for understanding its significance?

NAME ....

Focus on Setting

1. What is an example of a general setting?

a. A hotel in Chicago on July 5, 1981

b. Christmas Day, 1801

c. Midnight on September 1, 2002

d. California in the nineteenth century

2. Which of the following is a characteristic of an immediate setting?

a. Vague

b. General

c. Specific

d. Confusing

3. Which of the following best describes a story's mood?

a. The feeling the story creates in the reader

b. A symbol

c. A theme

d. A conflict

4. Which reading tool is useful for exploring the way setting and characters influence each other?

a. Timeline

b. Inference Chart

c. Outline

d. Key Word or Topic Notes

5. What do changes in setting usually signal?

a. Humor

b. The climax

c. Changes in action and atmosphere

d. None of the above

NAME ....

Focus on Characters

1. What is the difference between a protagonist and an antagonist?

....

....

....

2. What is the difference between round characters and flat characters?

....

....

....

3. What are three kinds of clues authors give to readers about what

characters are like?

....

....

....

4. What do you call a character who changes and grows over the course

of the story?

....

....

....

5. How can you use an Inference Chart to help you understand the

characters of a story?

....

....

NAME ....

Focus on Characters

1. Which of the following is an attribute of an antagonist?
   a. This person or thing works against the protagonist.
   b. This person or thing works with the protagonist.
   c. This person or thing is full of virtue.
   d. This person or thing is full of hate.

2. Which of the following best describes a static character?
   a. A major character
   b. A character who doesn't change
   c. An evil character
   d. A dynamic character

3. Which of the following is NOT a technique that authors use to create a character?
   a. Physical appearance
   b. Interactions with other characters
   c. Immediate settings
   d. Direct comments by the author

4. Which of the following best describes the relationship between character and plot?
   a. The plot has little influence on characters.
   b. The characters have no impact on the plot.
   c. The characters fulfill the plot.
   d. The plot shapes what characters do.

5. Which reading tool would you use if you want to focus on how a character changes?
   a. Plot Diagram
   b. Character Map
   c. Fiction Organizer
   d. Character Development Chart

NAME ....

Focus on Theme

1. What is a theme? ....

   ....

   ....

   ....

2. What is the three-step plan for finding the theme in a literary work?

   ....

   ....

   ....

3. What are three common topics for themes? ....

   ....

   ....

   ....

4. How can a Double-entry Journal help you understand the theme of a

   literary work? ....

   ....

   ....

   ....

5. Why is theme important? ....

   ....

   ....

   ....

NAME ....

Focus on Theme

1. Which is a good tip for writing a theme statement?
   a. Use at least two characters' names.
   b. Avoid using characters' names.
   c. Summarize the story.
   d. Avoid complete sentences.

2. What is the first step of the three-step plan for finding the theme in a literary work?
   a. Find out what the characters say.
   b. State what the author says about life.
   c. Skim.
   d. Identify the big ideas.

3. Which of the following is NOT a common topic for the theme?
   a. Friendship
   b. Love
   c. Biology
   d. War

4. Where are clues about the theme likely to appear?
   a. In important plot events
   b. In symbols
   c. In changes in characters' actions or beliefs
   d. All of the above

5. Which reading tool records the big ideas of a story and details what characters do and say?
   a. Topic and Theme Organizer
   b. Double-entry Journal
   c. Character Web
   d. Outline

NAME

Focus on Dialogue

1. What is dialogue?

2. How is dialogue typically indicated?

3. What is a good reading strategy to use when focusing on dialogue?

4. How does dialogue help readers better understand a character?

5. How can dialogue help readers understand the background of a story?

NAME

Focus on Dialogue

1. How does a writer often indicate who spoke certain dialogue?

   a. With capital letters

   b. In a list of characters

   c. By using speech tags

   d. By using parentheses

2. When are single quotation marks used with dialogue?

   a. When the quote is long

   b. When a character quotes what another character said

   c. When a new paragraph begins

   d. All of the above

3. What is a good reading strategy to use when focusing on dialogue?

   a. Close reading

   b. Skimming

   c. Proofreading

   d. Editing

4. How does dialogue often help readers better understand a character?

   a. It details the setting.

   b. It directly reveals the characters' ages.

   c. It reveals a character's feelings and personality.

   d. It explains the plot climax.

5. What would be an example of internal dialogue in a story?

   a. Characters talking about the past

   b. Dialogue with no speech tags

   c. An extended quotation spoken by the main character

   d. A conversation taking place in a character's mind

NAME ....

Focus on Comparing and Contrasting

1. What is the difference between comparing and contrasting?

....

....

....

2. What are three things you should look for as you preview two novels

before comparing them?

....

....

....

3. How does a Two-novel Map help you compare and contrast?

....

....

....

4. How can you use a Venn Diagram to compare and contrast?

....

....

....

5. What are three questions you can ask yourself to help you write a

comparison and contrast paper?

....

....

....

NAME

Focus on Comparing and Contrasting

1. What are you doing when you compare?

    a. Summarizing

    b. Focusing on how things are similar or different

    c. Focusing on how things are different

    d. Evaluating theme

2. What is a good strategy to use when you need to compare two different long novels?

    a. Close reading

    b. Paraphrasing

    c. Reading critically

    d. Using graphic organizers

3. How does a Two-novel Map help you to compare and contrast?

    a. It shows similarities and differences between two works.

    b. It tracks the dialogue in two novels.

    c. It organizes the symbols of each novel.

    d. It maps the location of each novel.

4. A Venn Diagram takes which of the following shapes?

    a. Two overlapping circles

    b. Two squares

    c. Two triangles and a circle.

    d. Three rectangles

5. Which of the following is generally NOT a question you may want to ask yourself when writing a comparison and contrast paper?

    a. Which work is longer?

    b. What were some key aspects of the styles?

    c. How believable were the plots?

    d. What were some important themes?

NAME

Elements of Fiction

1. How are an antagonist and a protagonist different?

2. What is characterization?

3. What are three common types of conflict in fictional works?

4. What is foreshadowing, and why might an author use it in a story?

5. How are the five parts of a classic plot organized?

NAME ....

Elements of Fiction

1. Which term refers to an author's attitude toward the subject, characters, or reader?
   a. Theme
   b. Tone
   c. Mood
   d. Style

2. Which of the following describes first-person point of view?
   a. Uses words such as *I, me, we,* or *my*
   b. Uses a narrator who isn't part of the story's action
   c. Features an omniscient narrator
   d. All of the above

3. Which of the following is NOT a main element of a writer's style?
   a. Word choice
   b. Sentence structure and length
   c. Literary devices
   d. Complication

4. What is an example of a genre?
   a. Theme statements
   b. Foreshadowing
   c. Science fiction
   d. Dialect

5. What is the first part of a plot?
   a. Exposition
   b. Rising action
   c. Falling action
   d. Resolution

NAME ....

Reading a Poem

1. Why is reading a poem more than once necessary? ....

....

....

....

2. Why is close reading a good strategy for reading poetry? ....

....

....

....

3. What do you do when you paraphrase a poem? ....

....

....

....

4. How does a Double-entry Journal help you interact with the poem as

you read? ....

....

....

....

5. How would you describe a sonnet? ....

....

....

....

NAME

Reading a Poem

1. What should you look for when you preview a poem?

a. Any rhymes

b. The first and last lines

c. The structure and shape of the poem on the page

d. All of the above

2. How do you mark the rhyme scheme of a poem?

a. With paraphrases and quotation marks

b. With underlining

c. With numbers

d. With letters

3. What is paraphrasing?

a. Offering your opinion

b. Reading out loud

c. Restating in your own words

d. Summarizing in paragraphs

4. What is free verse?

a. Poetry that follows no particular rules

b. A kind of long narrative poem

c. Poetry that stirs your emotions with rhymes

d. All of the above

5. What should you concentrate on when you read a poem for mood?

a. The meter

b. The feeling within the poem

c. The imagery and symbolism

d. The stanza organization

NAME ....

Focus on Language

1. How would you define tone? ....

....

....

....

2. What is the difference between a word's denotation and its

connotation? ....

....

....

....

3. What is figurative language, and what are some examples of figurative

language? ....

....

....

....

4. Why do poets often use imagery? ....

....

....

....

5. Why is close reading a good strategy to use when focusing on a

poem's language? ....

....

....

NAME ....

Focus on Language

1. What is a good strategy to use when focusing on poetic language?
   a. Skimming
   b. Close denotation
   c. Close reading
   d. Reading critically

2. What is a symbol?
   a. A big object
   b. Something concrete that stands for something abstract
   c. A point the author stresses
   d. A metaphor

3. Which of the following is NOT an example of figurative language?
   a. Fact
   b. Simile
   c. Metaphor
   d. Symbol

4. Why do poets often use imagery?
   a. To complicate a rhyme scheme
   b. To create boredom
   c. To create a stanza
   d. To stimulate senses

5. Which of the following is an example of a simile?
   a. "An eerie, dark hallway"
   b. "Excited as a toddler in a toy store"
   c. "Blowing gently, swaying slowly"
   d. None of the above

NAME

Focus on Meaning

1. What is the difference between the subject of a poem and its
meaning?

2. How can looking at denotations and connotations help you
understand a poem?

3. Why are close reading and paraphrasing good strategies for
understanding a poem?

4. How does a Double-entry Journal help you understand a poem?

5. How can listening to your own feelings help you understand a poem?

NAME

Focus on Meaning

1. What do you do when you paraphrase a line of a poem?
   a. Put the meaning into your own words.
   b. Evaluate the figurative language.
   c. Analyze the style.
   c. Quote the key words.

2. Which is true of the connotation of a word?
   a. The connotation is your emotional response to the word.
   b. The connotation is the dictionary definition.
   c. The connotation is a metaphor.
   d. Each word has only one connotation.

3. What are two good strategies for understanding a poem?
   a. Skimming and outlining
   b. Planning and revising
   c. Close reading and paraphrasing
   d. Previewing and summarizing

4. When you write down your thoughts about words from the poem and their meaning, what tool do you use?
   a. Double-entry Journal
   b. Topic and Theme Organizer
   c. Main Idea Organizer
   d. Story String

5. What should you pay particular attention to when you're focusing on the meaning of a poem?
   a. The first and last several lines
   b. The title
   c. Words that express strong emotion
   d. All of the above

NAME

Focus on Sound and Structure

1. What is meant by the structure of a poem?

2. Which strategy can you use to focus on the sound and structure of a poem?

3. What is alliteration?

4. What is assonance?

5. What is the rhythm of a poem?

NAME ....

Focus on Sound and Structure

1. What do stanza divisions of a poem often signal?

a. The use of alliteration

b. The beginning of a new thought or image

c. Irregular rhythm

d. The lack of rhyme

2. How would you mark the rhyme scheme of a four-line poem in which lines 1 and 3 rhyme?

a. abcd

b. 1, 2, 1, 3

c. abab

d. abac

3. Which of the following is an example of alliteration?

a. "Cool, calm cucumber"

b. "Mad, sad, glad"

c. "Lazy, crazy day"

d. None of the above

4. What is assonance? Describe it.

a. Repetition of beginning consonant sounds

b. Repetition of vowel sounds

c. End rhyme

d. Figurative language

5. The "meter" of a poem refers to which of the following?

a. The length of each line

b. The length of each stanza

c. The poem's beat or rhythm

d. The poem's repeated sounds

NAME

Elements of Poetry

1. What is onomatopoeia?

2. How is a metaphor different from a simile?

3. What is tone?

4. What is personification?

5. What is hyperbole?

Elements of Poetry

1. Which of the following is an example of onomatopoeia?

    a. "White dove"

    b. "Easy as pie"

    c. "Bang!"

    d. "Happy hippo hugs"

2. "Heart like cold stone" is an example of what?

    a. Metaphor

    b. Simile

    c. Alliteration

    d. Inversion

3. What is the repetition of identical consonant sounds that are preceded by different vowel sounds?

    a. Consonance

    b. Allusion

    c. Mood

    d. Personification

4. What is language that appeals to the senses?

    a. Personification

    b. Imagery

    c. Voice

    d. Tone

5. What is true of stanzas?

    a. They can be of different lengths.

    b. They are like paragraphs in prose.

    c. White space often separates one from another.

    d. All of the above

NAME

Reading a Play

1. What are two unique features in a play that separate it from novels and stories?

2. How does summarizing help you read a play?

3. How is a play organized?

4. What is a Plot Diagram, and how is it useful for reading a play?

5. Why is visualizing and thinking aloud a good strategy for rereading plays?

NAME ....

Reading a Play

1. Which feature separates a play from a novel or story?

a. Plot

b. Stage directions

c. Characters

d. Theme

2. Which tool organizes information around key concepts or words?

a. Character Map

b. Timeline

c. Magnet Summary

d. Making Connections Chart

3. How are plays organized?

a. In chapters

b. In sections

c. In outline format

d. In acts and scenes

4. Why is a Plot Diagram helpful for reading a play?

a. It helps you understand the characters.

b. It helps you understand the events of the play.

c. It helps you find the symbols in the play.

d. It helps you find the topic of the play.

5. In many cases, what does a scene change indicate?

a. A change in the time or place

b. A monologue

c. A theme statement

d. The entrance of the main character

NAME ....

Focus on Language

1. What are three elements that can help you understand the language

of a play?

2. Why are stage directions important in a play?

3. What are two purposes dialogue serves in a play?

4. How does an Inference Chart help you understand the play?

5. What reading tool can you use to help you remember the key

passages after reading a play?

Focus on Language

1. Which of the following is NOT an element of language that can help you understand a play?
   a. Length of sentences
   b. Key lines and speeches
   c. Stage directions
   d. Dialogue as a clue to character, plot, and theme

2. Which of the following tells actors how to perform the play?
   a. Cast of characters
   b. Theme
   c. Stage directions
   d. Dialogue

3. Dialogue serves which of the following purposes in a play?
   a. Establishes alliteration
   b. Tells you about the playwright's life
   c. Makes the play shorter
   d. Advances the plot

4. Which of the following helps you keep a record of your conclusions?
   a. Outline
   b. Inference Chart
   c. Character Web
   d. Plot Diagram

5. How might dialogue reveal a playwright's themes?
   a. Someone makes a strong statement about society.
   b. A character talks about a deep insight.
   c. A character talks about a change in himself or herself.
   d. All of the above

NAME ....

Focus on Theme

1. What is theme?

....

....

....

2. What is a good plan for understanding theme?

....

....

....

3. How does a Topic and Theme Organizer help you understand a play?

....

....

....

4. What is the difference between a topic and a theme?

....

....

....

5. How can you use a Main Idea Organizer when you're focusing on a

play's theme?

....

....

....

NAME

Focus on Theme

1. Which of the following best describes theme?

   a. The playwright's message for the audience

   b. The main symbol of the play

   c. The concluding sentence of the play

   d. The most important passage of the play

2. What is the first step of the plan for understanding theme?

   a. State the theme.

   b. Notice the dialogue of the characters.

   c. Find the general topic of the play.

   d. Take note of the characters' actions.

3. Which of the following is a good method to help you keep track of your thoughts about the big ideas in a play?

   a. Timeline

   b. Character Web

   c. Storyboard

   d. Topic and Theme Organizer

4. What is the difference between a topic and a theme?

   a. There is no difference.

   b. The theme is the author's message about the topic.

   c. The topic is the author's message about the theme.

   d. The theme is shorter in length than the topic.

5. What part of a play should you pay attention to when you're looking for clues about themes?

   a. Where characters learn something about themselves

   b. Where characters learn something about life

   c. Where characters learn something about others

   d. All of the above

NAME

Focus on Shakespeare

1. What are some reasons why reading a play by Shakespeare is challenging?

2. What are the two steps of the reading plan for Shakespeare?

3. How can Summary Notes help you understand a Shakespearean play?

4. What is one tip for understanding Shakespeare?

5. What are two recurring topics in Shakespeare's plays?

NAME ....

Focus on Shakespeare

1. Why are Shakespeare's plays challenging?

a. They have three acts.

b. They have twenty characters each.

c. They include unfamiliar words and have a challenging style.

d. The themes of his plays no longer apply to life today.

2. What is the first step of reading a Shakespearean play?

a. Skim the entire play.

b. Reread key scenes.

c. Analyze all the characters.

d. Read the entire play for sense.

3. What is blank verse?

a. Dialogue spoken by servants

b. Poetry with a regular rhythm

c. Poetry about love

d. All of the above

4. Which of the following is an example of an inverted line?

a. "Then was the moon bright."

b. "The stars were ne'er shining."

c. "She dost understand thee well."

d. "Thou should leave."

5. In which of the following can you record your reaction to your favorite lines?

a. Character Map

b. Paraphrase Chart

c. Web

d. Timeline

NAME ....

Elements of Drama

1. How are plays often divided?

....

....

....

2. How does a chorus contribute to the action of a play?

....

....

....

3. What are stage directions?

....

....

....

4. What's the difference between a monologue and an aside?

....

....

....

5. How does a subplot differ from the plot of a play?

....

....

....

NAME

Elements of Drama

1. What are smaller sections of acts called?

    a. Stanzas

    b. Scenes

    c. Key lines

    d. Stage directions

2. What is a chorus?

    a. A single actor who makes a speech

    b. A major division in a play

    c. A group of actors who speak together

    d. The actors who sing at the end of an act

3. Which of the following things do stage directions NOT describe?

    a. Lighting

    b. Instructions to actors

    c. Notes on props and costumes

    d. What the actors say

4. What section of a play contains a list of characters?

    a. Speech tags

    b. Dialogue

    c. Cast of characters

    d. Act

5. Which of these things is true of a soliloquy?

    a. It is like a monologue.

    b. It is a kind of subplot.

    c. It involves many characters speaking as one voice.

    d. It is an important part of the stage directions.

NAME

Reading a Website

1. When you read a website, what should you do first?

2. What are three things to look for when previewing a website?

3. Why is reading critically an important strategy when reading a website?

4. What is skimming, and what is a good tip for skimming a site?

5. Why is a Website Profiler a good tool to organize what you learned on a website?

Reading a Website

1. What is a search engine?

a. A link

b. A general URL

c. A program that helps you find information

d. A program that finds spelling errors

2. Which of the following is NOT something to look for when previewing a website?

a. Source or sponsor

b. Main menu or table of contents

c. Bibliography

d. Name of website and overall appearance

3. Which of the following helps you evaluate the website's credibility?

a. Outlining

b. Visualizing

c. Skimming

d. Reading critically

4. What is a good tip for skimming?

a. Read everything.

b. Look for supporting details.

c. Read slowly.

d. Do NOT read everything.

5. Which is true of the organization of websites?

a. It is similar to the organization of books.

b. It is different from the organization of books.

c. It is always in chronological order.

d. None of the above

NAME ....

Elements of the Internet

1. How do you use a search engine? ....

....

....

....

2. The header of an email usually includes which four elements? ....

....

....

....

3. What is a newsgroup? ....

....

....

....

4. What is the World Wide Web? ....

....

....

....

5. What are three common elements of a website? ....

....

....

....

NAME ....

Elements of the Internet

1. Which of the following is a good tip for using email wisely?

a. Use all capital letters to express emotion.

b. Be cautious about giving out personal information.

c. Give your home phone number when you are in a chat room.

d. All of the above

2. Which of these things does NOT appear in the header of an email?

a. The message

b. The subject

c. The sender's address

d. The date and time the message was sent

3. An online discussion area can also be called which of the following?

a. Newsgroup

b. Search engine

c. Database

d. Link

4. What is a URL?

a. United Record List

b. Unified Recording Locator

c. Uniform Resource Locator

d. United Registration List

5. Which of the following takes you from one website page to another?

a. Features

b. Home page

c. Browser

d. Link

NAME

Reading a Graphic

1. What are three things that you should look for when previewing a graphic?

2. What are the five steps of the plan for reading a graphic?

3. Why is paraphrasing a good reading strategy for graphics?

4. Why is a Critical Reading Chart a good tool for reading graphics?

5. How do you find the axes and the legend of a graphic?

NAME ....

Reading a Graphic

1. Which of the following should you NOT look for when you preview a graphic?

   a. Any keys or legends

   b. Any conclusions you can draw

   c. Any labels

   d. The scale or unit of measurement

2. What is the first step for reading a graphic?

   a. Scan the graphic.

   b. Make a connection with the graphic.

   c. Question the data.

   d. Paraphrase the information.

3. Which of the following is a good strategy for putting information into your own words?

   a. Questioning the author

   b. Skimming

   c. Outlining

   d. Paraphrasing

4. What is a tool for reading graphics that helps you draw conclusions about the reliability of a graphic?

   a. Argument Chart

   b. Plot Diagram

   c. Critical Reading Chart

   d. Making a Connections Chart

5. Which of the following explains the different colors and symbols on a graphic?

   a. Horizontal axis

   b. Vertical axis

   c. Legend

   d. Title

NAME

Elements of Graphics

1. What is a cartoon?

2. What does a flow chart show?

3. What are two kinds of maps, and what does each show?

4. What does a pie chart show?

5. How would you describe the purpose of a timeline?

Elements of Graphics

1. What does a bar graph do?

   a. Plots data in two circles

   b. Compares quantities, amounts, groups, or time periods

   c. Show parts of a whole in one circle

   d. None of the above

2. What does a line graph show?

   a. Points plotted and connected to show change over time

   b. Percentages of the whole

   c. The time order of a process

   d. Physical features of land

3. Which of the following is NOT a type of map?

   a. Political

   b. Demographic

   c. Physical

   d. Vertical

4. Which graphic shows the relative size or importance of different factors?

   a. Timeline

   b. Cartoon

   c. Pie chart

   d. Thematic Map

5. What should you look at first when you read a table?

   a. The key

   b. The conclusion

   c. The title and any captions

   d. The labels of the two axes

NAME

Reading a Driver's Handbook

1. What are some things to preview when reading a driver's handbook?

2. Why is skimming a good reading strategy for reading a driver's handbook?

3. Why are Summary Notes a good reading tool for reading a driver's handbook?

4. How do Key Word or Topic Notes help you organize information?

5. What should you ask yourself after you've finished reading?

Reading a Driver's Handbook

1. Which of the following should you look for when previewing a driver's handbook?
   a. Supporting details
   b. Captions
   c. Table of contents
   d. Concluding sentence

2. What do you do when you skim?
   a. Read every word.
   b. Look at pictures only.
   c. Move your eyes quickly over the page.
   d. Make important inferences.

3. What is a good strategy to use when you reread?
   a. Previewing
   b. Visualizing and thinking aloud
   c. Setting a purpose
   d. Paraphrasing

4. Which reading tools help you remember everyday reading material?
   a. Summary Notes and Webs
   b. Webs and Fiction Organizers
   c. Inference Charts and Character Maps
   d. Argument Charts and Plot Diagrams

5. Why should you connect everyday reading to your own life?
   a. To appreciate style
   b. To remember what you've read
   c. To recognize themes
   d. To skim more quickly

NAME

Focus on Reading Instructions

1. How do you set a purpose for reading instructions?

2. What is one reading strategy that is useful for reading instructions?

3. What are two practices that are helpful for a close reading of instructions?

4. How does thinking aloud help when you read instructions?

5. What are two things you might try if the instructions don't work for you the first time?

NAME ....

Focus on Reading Instructions

1. Which is NOT something to look for when previewing reading instructions?

   a. Any diagrams or graphics

   b. Any bulleted lists

   c. The main idea sentence

   d. Any key words in boldface

2. Which of the following is a useful reading strategy for reading instructions?

   a. Questioning the author

   b. Reading critically

   c. Close reading

   d. Outlining

3. Which of the following is the first step in a close reading of instructions?

   a. Making personal connections

   b. Highlighting important words or phrases

   c. Reading diagrams

   d. Rereading

4. Why is it important to reread instructions?

   a. It helps you understand the information.

   b. The diagrams are nice to look at.

   c. You can make different notes.

   d. All of the above

5. What is a good suggestion for reading instructions?

   a. Do one step at a time.

   b. Reread as necessary.

   c. Pay close attention to diagrams.

   d. All of the above

NAME ....

Focus on Reading for Work

1. What are the four steps for understanding workplace reading? ....
   ....
   ....
   ....

2. How do you set a purpose for reading work-related material?
   ....
   ....
   ....

3. What is one reading strategy that is useful for reading for work? ....

   Why? ....
   ....
   ....
   ....

4. What is one tip for skimming workplace reading effectively? ....
   ....
   ....
   ....

5. What are two things you might try if you can't find what you need

   in the reading material? ....
   ....
   ....
   ....

NAME ....

Focus on Reading for Work

1. What is the first step for reading at work?

   a. Preview the material.

   b. Identify the reason you're reading.

   c. Apply the information to your own life.

   d. Talk to your supervisor.

2. Which of the following is a useful reading strategy for reading in the workplace?

   a. Reading critically

   b. Skimming

   c. Questioning the author

   d. Visualizing and thinking aloud

3. Which of the following is a good practice for skimming information at work?

   a. Reading titles or headings

   b. Highlighting key passages and words

   c. Connecting the information to yourself

   d. All of the above

4. Why is it most important to connect to work-related reading material?

   a. It will get you promoted.

   b. It's NOT really important to connect to the information.

   c. It helps you understand the information.

   d. It gives you something to talk about with co-workers.

5. How might work-related reading be organized?

   a. With numbered steps

   b. By times

   c. By dates

   d. All of the above

NAME ....

Reading Tests and Test Questions

1. What are the three steps for answering test questions? ....

....

....

....

2. Why is skimming a good reading strategy to use when taking tests? ....

....

....

....

3. What are the three basic types of test questions? ....

....

....

....

4. What is one reading tool you can use to answer essay questions? ....

....

....

....

5. What can you do to reflect on a particular test you've just taken? ....

....

....

....

Reading Tests and Test Questions

1. What should you look for when you preview a test?

a. Instructions about marking answers

b. The amount of time you have

c. Whether there is a penalty for wrong answers

d. All of the above

2. Which of the following is NOT a major type of test question?

a. Essay

b. Factual recall

c. Critical thinking

d. Theme

3. How can you find important information for factual recall questions on tests?

a. By skimming and looking for key words

b. By looking at the notes that you brought with you

c. By asking your teacher

d. By trying to remember what you studied

4. Which of the following reading tools can help you plan your answer to an essay question?

a. Main Idea Organizer

b. Character Development Chart

c. Inference Chart

d. Story String

5. How are test questions often organized?

a. From hardest to easiest

b. From easiest to hardest

c. From longest to shortest

d. In chronological order

NAME

Focus on English Tests

1. What are two tips for preparing to take an English test?

2. What are two ways to improve your vocabulary?

3. What do word analogies test?

4. What is the process for previewing and taking an English test?

5. What kinds of questions are you likely to find on an English test?

NAME ....

Focus on English Tests

1. Which of the following reading tools is useful in learning new vocabulary words?
   a. Main Idea Organizer
   b. Study Cards
   c. Fiction Organizer
   d. Outline

2. Which of the following is NOT a type of question found on an English test?
   a. Word problem questions
   b. Reading passage questions
   c. Vocabulary questions
   d. Grammar, usage, and mechanics questions

3. Which of the following is an example of an antonym word analogy?
   a. Up: down
   b. Spring: summer
   c. Red: white
   d. None of the above

4. What's important to look for when previewing an English test?
   a. Diagrams
   b. The length of each question
   c. The types of questions on the test
   d. The number of pages in the test

5. What is a good strategy to use when answering reading passage questions?
   a. Reading critically
   b. Skimming
   c. Outlining
   d. Questioning the author

NAME

Focus on Writing Tests

1. What basic areas are usually covered on a writing test?

2. What are two tips for getting ready to take a writing test?

3. What are the three parts your essay should include?

4. What are the three common kinds of writing prompts?

5. What is a good reading tool to use in preparing to write for a test?

NAME

Focus on Writing Tests

1. Which is NOT a basic area covered on a writing test?
   a. Answering word problems
   b. Responding to essay questions in timed writings
   c. Improving sentences and paragraphs
   d. Correcting sentence errors

2. Which of the following is a good way to prepare for a writing test?
   a. Talk to others who have taken the test before.
   b. Complete a practice test.
   c. Review basic rules for correcting sentence errors.
   d. All of the above

3. What is the first step of the writing plan for responding to prompts?
   a. Writing the topic sentence
   b. Proofreading
   c. Concluding the essay
   d. Supporting the topic sentence

4. What reading tool could be helpful in preparing a response to a writing prompt?
   a. Main Idea Organizer
   b. Story Organizer
   c. Topic and Theme Organizer
   d. Double-entry Journal

5. After you finish writing your essay, you should _____.
   a. Reread to make sure the content is clear.
   b. Check for errors in grammar.
   c. Ask yourself if you've answered the question clearly.
   d. All of the above

NAME

Focus on Standardized Tests

1. What are the two tips for preparing to take a standardized test?

2. Why is it important to preview a standardized test before taking it?

3. What is a good reading strategy to use with standardized test questions?

4. What are two tips for spotting wrong answers to test questions?

5. At the end of a test, you should use the last two minutes to do what?

NAME

Focus on Standardized Tests

1. Which of the following are ways to prepare for standardized tests?
   a. Relaxing
   b. Taking a practice test
   c. Visiting the test website
   d. All of the above

2. What should you look for when previewing a standardized test?
   a. The name of the company that publishes the test
   b. The number of pages in the test booklet
   c. The easiest questions
   d. Words you don't already know

3. Which of the following is good advice for reading test questions?
   a. Mark important points with a highlighter.
   b. Think about several questions at a time.
   c. Don't read every word.
   d. All of the above

4. Which of the following is a good strategy for making educated guesses when answering difficult questions?
   a. Reading critically
   b. Questioning the author
   c. Outlining
   d. Visualizing and thinking aloud

5. When you're done with your test, what should you do before time runs out?
   a. Reread all the directions.
   b. Go back and check your work.
   c. Worry about how you did.
   d. Erase any marks you made when previewing.

NAME

Focus on History Tests

1. What are two good ways to prepare for a history test?

2. How do you preview a history test?

3. What is a "top ten list" you might create for a history test?

4. What can you do if you're unsure of an answer to a question?

5. What's the first thing you should do when you come to a graphic on a history test?

NAME ....

Focus on History Tests

1. History tests focus on which of the following?
   a. Knowledge of current cultural events
   b. Knowledge of important events and their dates
   c. Knowledge of scientific processes
   d. Knowledge of word analogies

2. Which is true of most visuals on a history test?
   a. They have no title.
   b. The text is more important than the graphics.
   c. The graphics and text are equally important.
   d. The graphics are more important than the text.

3. Which of the following is NOT an example of graphics?
   a. Maps
   b. Timelines
   c. Political cartoons
   d. Famous documents

4. After previewing a test, which questions should you answer first?
   a. The easiest questions
   b. The hardest questions
   c. Questions with graphs
   d. Questions with diagrams

5. Which is good advice for answering a multiple-choice question?
   a. Read all the answers before making a choice.
   b. Try to eliminate incorrect answers.
   c. Begin by answering the easiest questions.
   d. All of the above

NAME

Focus on Math Tests

1. What is a good way to prepare for a math test?

2. What should you do when you preview a math test?

3. When working through math problems, how does visualizing help?

4. What does it mean to "plug in" answer choices?

5. After finishing a test, what should you do?

NAME ....

Focus on Math Tests

1. Which of the following is a good way to prepare for a math test?

a. Reread your math book cover to cover.

b. Review old assignments and tests.

c. Practice using a calculator.

d. Highlight the key words in questions.

2. Which is NOT a good test-taking technique to use with hard questions?

a. Trying easier numbers first

b. Visualizing the answer

c. Plugging in answers

d. Highlighting all the words in a question

3. When you get the test, what should you do first?

a. Take two minutes to scan the entire test.

b. Work beginning to end until finished.

c. Work end to beginning until finished.

d. Begin in the middle of the test.

4. What should you look for when previewing a math test?

a. The tricky answers

b. The kinds of questions

c. The number of pages

d. The number of questions about geometry

5. What does it mean to visualize an answer?

a. To guess

b. To preview the directions

c. To sketch or draw to help make a problem clearer

d. To check the math with a calculator

NAME

Focus on Science Tests

1. What can you do to learn science terms?

2. When you preview a science test, what should you do?

3. What is one strategy that will help you answer the questions on

science tests?

4. What are the three steps in answering a science reasoning question?

5. What does making an educated guess involve?

Focus on Science Tests

1. Many science tests are divided into which two parts?
   - a. Science knowledge and science reasoning
   - b. Science facts and memorization
   - c. Formulas and experiments
   - d. None of the above

2. What does it mean to make an educated guess?
   - a. Filling in ovals on the answer sheet at random
   - b. Choosing partially true statements
   - c. Looking for clues and eliminating wrong answers
   - d. Skipping the question

3. Which of the following strategies will help you answer science test questions?
   - a. Outlining
   - b. Reading critically
   - c. Questioning the author
   - d. Visualizing and thinking aloud

4. Previewing the test involves all but which of the following?
   - a. Skimming the directions
   - b. Marking the easy questions
   - c. Rechecking your class notes
   - d. Glancing at any charts and diagrams

5. What types of questions are found on science tests?
   - a. Multiple-choice
   - b. True-false
   - c. Essay
   - d. All of the above

NAME

Improving Vocabulary

1. What are three ways to increase your vocabulary?

2. What are three types of context clues?

3. What is a word root? Give an example.

4. What is the difference between a suffix and a prefix?

5. What's the definition of analogy? Give an example of an analogy.

NAME ....

Improving Vocabulary

1. Which is NOT recorded in a vocabulary journal?

   a. The unfamiliar word

   b. The definition

   c. The connotations and history of the unfamiliar word

   d. A sentence or phrase using the unfamiliar word

2. What is the part of the word that carries its meaning?

   a. Word root

   b. Prefix

   c. Suffix

   d. Context clue

3. Which of the following words contains at least one prefix?

   a. Disconnect

   b. Semiconductor

   c. Precook

   d. All of the above

4. What's the purpose of the guidewords on a dictionary page?

   a. To help you locate the word you're looking for

   b. To give word histories

   c. To show how to pronounce words

   d. None of the above

5. Which of the following is a word analogy that shows a whole and part relationship?

   a. Dessert: pie

   b. Animals: elephant

   c. Flower: daisy

   d. Coat: sleeves

NAME ....

Doing Research

1. How are the reading process and the research process similar? ....

....

....

....

2. What is the difference between a primary source and a secondary

source? Give an example of each. ....

....

....

....

3. What is a good tool for evaluating a source? ....

....

....

....

4. Why is it important to use quotation marks and ellipses when you

quote from sources? ....

....

....

....

5. What is the difference between formal and informal documentation? ....

....

....

....

NAME ....

Doing Research

1. Which of the following is true about the research process?

   a. It includes the same steps as the reading process.

   b. It is totally different from the reading process.

   c. It involves fewer steps than the reading process.

   d. It has more steps than the reading process.

2. What of the following is NOT a primary source?

   a. Autobiography

   b. Memoir

   c. Letter

   d. Magazine

3. Where can you find secondary sources?

   a. At the library

   b. On the Internet

   c. At universities

   d. All of the above

4. What does the Dewey decimal system do?

   a. Rates books according to their credibility

   b. Labels search engines

   c. Divides books into subject categories

   d. Evaluates government publications

5. How can you find a particular article in a newspaper?

   a. By consulting an atlas

   b. By looking up the book's call number

   c. By using a periodical database

   d. All of the above

Answer Key

MULTIPLE CHOICE

CORRECT ANSWER

INTRODUCTION

Short-answer Test

1. *Answers may include three of the following:* We read to obtain information from academic materials, to find out about things that interest us personally, to keep up with work-related information and instructions, and to get information from functional materials, such as schedules and directions.

2. Reading and writing are both processes because they both consist of several steps.

3. Accept any of the items listed in the left column of the table on pages 30–32 of the *Reader's Handbook*.

4. *Answers may include one of the following:* Both reading and writing are processes made up of several steps. Both involve answering questions and making decisions as you work through the process. Both include an early stage in which you make a first draft or preread and gain a first impression and a later stage that involves "fixing up" the earlier draft or impression.

5. Possible answers include that technology has changed what we read by introducing messages on pagers and cell phones. People also read letters as email and instant messages. Books are available on audio as well as in print. Soon textbooks may be available in digital form.

Multiple-choice Test

1. b   **2.** c   **3.** a   **4.** b   **5.** d

THE READING PROCESS

Short-answer Test

1. The three main stages of the reading process are Before Reading, During Reading, and After Reading.

2. When you preview a reading, you skim it quickly, looking for information about vocabulary, organization, and content.

3. Useful questions to ask include the following: "How do I feel after reading this?" "Do I agree with the author's point of view? How does this affect me?" and "Have I read anything else by this author?"

4. Rereading helps you clear up confusing parts of a reading and experience the text in a new way.

5. Good readers can improve their ability to remember information by doing something to make the information their own. For example, they might write a summary of what they've read or talk about the information with someone else.

Multiple-choice Test

1. c   **2.** d   **3.** a   **4.** a   **5.** c

READING KNOW-HOW

Short-answer Test

1. When you make an inference, you put together what you learned from the reading with what you already know. Making an inference means reading "between the lines" to make a reasonable guess about meaning.

2. When you react and connect to a reading, you think about how it makes you feel and what it reminds you of in your own life.

3. To find the implied main idea of a paragraph, you must infer the writer's meaning from clues in the material. These clues may appear in a heading, the first sentence, details, or the last sentence. Once you find the subject, you need to use the clues to decide the point the author is making about it.

4. An expository paragraph offers information or explains something. This type of paragraph often presents facts, gives directions, and defines terms.

5. Paragraphs arranged in geographic order start with a description of a place and then move from that place to another in order to establish what is happening where in the story. Details may be arranged left to right, top to bottom, and so on.

Multiple-choice Test

1. d   **2.** c   **3.** c   **4.** a   **5.** b

READING HISTORY

Short-answer Test

1. *Answers may include three of the following:* the title, the list of terms and names and any introductory information; the first and last paragraphs of the chapter; the headings; any names, dates, words, or terms set in bold type or that are repeated; any bulleted lists; and any photos, maps, or pictures and their captions.

2. Two tools that are extremely useful for reading history are the 5 W's and H Organizer, which helps you keep track of basic information, and Key Word or Topic Notes, which helps you focus on key points in the reading. A Web can be useful to group details around key topics.

3. Texts arranged in chronological, or time, order tell what happened first, then what happened next, and then what happened after that. Texts arranged in geographical, or location, order discuss events in one area before going on to tell of events in another area.

4. Rereading gives you a chance to look for details you need to expand your notes and make concepts clearer.

5. It is a good idea to use graphic organizers, such as a Web, when rereading, to help you group details in a visual way. Graphic organizers help you retain more of what you read.

Multiple-choice Test

1. b   **2.** b   **3.** d   **4.** a   **5.** d

READING SCIENCE

Short-answer Test

1. *Answers may include three of the following:* the title, the first and last paragraphs of the chapter; the headings; any words set in bold type or that are repeated; any boxed material; any photos, charts, or pictures and their captions; and the list of objectives and any review questions.

2. Outlining is a good strategy to use when reading a science textbook. An Outline helps you understand the text's organization. Main topics are often numbered with Roman numerals; subtopics are given capital letters.

3. Rereading helps you remember and clarify what you've read.

4. *Answers may include one of the following:* an Outline, a Cause-Effect Organizer, Classification Notes, a Problem-Solution Organizer, and Study Cards.

5. Three common methods of organizing science writing are cause and effect, classification, and problem and solution.

Multiple-choice Test

1. a   **2.** a   **3.** d   **4.** d   **5.** b

READING MATH

Short-answer Test

1. *Answers may include three of the following:* the title; any listed goals; the introductory paragraph of the chapter; the headings, boldface words, color, and highlighted items; the models, diagrams, and examples; the boxed items; and the review questions.

2. Visualizing helps you take an abstract idea and turn it into a concrete image. Thinking aloud encourages you to "talk" to yourself about what you're thinking.

3. Most math texts are organized by chapters, with each chapter covering a major topic. Each chapter is divided into sections numbered with decimals: 1.1, 1.2, 1.3, and so on. Each decimal indicates a subheading. Each math chapter begins with an opening explanation, followed by sample problems, graphs and diagrams, and exercises.

4. Rereading helps you fully comprehend what you've read. You can go back to examples, exercises, or terms that seem confusing.

5. One good rereading strategy to use with math textbooks is note-taking.

Multiple-choice Test

1. d   **2.** d   **3.** b   **4.** a   **5.** b

FOCUS ON FOREIGN LANGUAGE

Short-answer Test

1. A foreign language textbook usually contains new vocabulary and grammar rules and assignments in speaking and writing the language.

2. Note-taking helps you memorize new vocabulary and understand and remember grammar rules.

3. Either Study Cards or a Web works well with a foreign language textbook. Both help you keep track of information and organize it visually.

4. *Idiom* refers to an expression that cannot be understood by the individual meanings of the words in the expression.

5. Three methods of reviewing a foreign language text include looking at notes or organizers, playing a game, or making up a practice test.

Multiple-choice Test
1. d　　　**2.** b　　　**3.** a　　　**4.** b　　　**5.** d

FOCUS ON SCIENCE CONCEPTS

Short-answer Test

1. *Answers may include three of the following:* the title and headings; the first paragraph; the objectives; any photos and their captions; any key terms and ideas set in boldface; and any bulleted lists.

2. Many science concepts involve vocabulary you'll want to remember and a process or series of steps to read about or to follow.

3. A Flow Chart shows processes or a sequence of steps in a visual way.

4. Two ways of reviewing information are reviewing your Flow Chart or Outline of the material and having a conversation about the information with another student.

5. A science concept is another word for a general scientific idea. Specific examples will vary, but might include *energy*, *scientific method*, or *mitosis*.

Multiple-choice Test
1. a　　　**2.** b　　　**3.** c　　　**4.** a　　　**5.** d

FOCUS ON STUDY QUESTIONS

Short-answer Test

1. The four-step plan for answering study questions includes the following steps: read, plan, write, and reread and edit.

2. A good strategy for reading study questions is visualizing and thinking aloud, which lets you focus on what the question means. It involves talking through what you need to do to answer the question and, if appropriate, making a sketch or a picture.

3. In study questions, *evaluate* means to judge or determine the worth or value of something.

4. Marking up a question helps you see the key words and concepts in a question.

5. If you have trouble answering a difficult study question, you can either talk over the question with a partner or you can review the chapter and section introductions as well as any material labeled "preview," "summary," or "review."

Multiple-choice Test

1. d   **2.** d   **3.** c   **4.** b   **5.** a

FOCUS ON WORD PROBLEMS

Short-answer Test

1. The four-step plan for solving word problems includes the following steps: read, plan, solve, and check.

2. The strategy of visualizing and thinking aloud works well with word problems. Visualizing a problem helps you see relationships between items in the problem, and thinking aloud gives you an opportunity to talk through the solution to the problem.

3. Solving a problem in another way involves using a different strategy than you used originally. For example, if you used a Think Aloud to solve a problem, try solving it again using a calculator to check your work.

4. Estimating with simpler numbers involves rounding the numbers in the problem and refiguring in order to check your work. If the new answer is close to your original answer, then the original is probably correct.

5. Sharing ideas, notes, and sketches with a partner will make the ideas clearer to both of you.

Multiple-choice Test

1. b   **2.** d   **3.** c   **4.** a   **5.** d

ELEMENTS OF TEXTBOOKS

Short-answer Test

1. Chapter previews are brief sections at the beginning of chapters that give you an idea of what you will be reading.

2. Charts give information, show processes, or make comparisons, often in column form, while graphs use lines, symbols, and pictures to show information.

3. Footnotes are numbered notes or comments at the bottom or side of a page, referring to something on the page.

4. Glossaries are arranged in alphabetical order.

5. *Typography* refers to the type styles, or fonts, used on a page.

Multiple-choice Test
1. b **2.** c **3.** d **4.** b **5.** d

READING A PERSONAL ESSAY

Short-answer Test

1. *Answers may include two of the following:* What is the subject of the essay? What does the writer say about the subject? How do I feel about what the writer says?

2. When previewing an essay, you should look at the title and author's name; the first and last paragraphs; any key words or any words in boldface or italics; and any repeated words or phrases.

3. Outlining is useful when reading a personal essay. It gives you a chance to see how the information in the essay is related to the main idea and helps you decide what's important and what's not important.

4. Most personal essays are organized in a funnel pattern. It consists of a several-paragraph topic introduction, the body, and a brief conclusion.

5. You might decide to reread a personal essay to clarify your understanding of what the author says about the subject. Questioning the author is a good rereading strategy to use.

Multiple-choice Test
1. d **2.** b **3.** a **4.** c **5.** b

READING AN EDITORIAL

Short-answer Test

1. You can identify the author's viewpoint in an editorial by reading actively, looking for assertions, and by using the strategy of questioning the author. Ask yourself, "What point is the author making?"

2. Questioning the author involves setting purpose questions before reading an editorial and then thinking about those questions as you read. While reading, you jot down answers in your reading journal and then use those answers to reach conclusions about what the writer is saying in the editorial.

3. A Critical Reading Chart helps you evaluate information in a piece of writing. It focuses on the evidence and sources and their reliability.

4. *Answers may include one of the following:* a Double-entry Journal, a Critical Reading Chart, or an Inference Chart.

5. An editorial is usually organized in three parts: assertions, support, and recommendation.

Multiple-choice Test
1. b   **2.** b   **3.** a   **4.** b   **5.** d

READING A NEWS STORY

Short-answer Test

1. You are most likely to find information about the *who, what, where, when, why,* and *how* in the headline and first paragraph of a news story.

2. Reading critically means looking at the facts presented by the writer and deciding what those facts mean and how believable they are. In addition, critical readers evaluate evidence, deciding if it is convincing, and think about what information may have been left out of the story.

3. A Critical Reading Chart is a good reading tool to use when reading critically. The chart helps you locate, keep track of, and evaluate the most important details or evidence in a story.

4. After you finish reading, it's a good idea to think about what you've learned. Consider you've met your purpose, how well you understand the main idea and facts, and whether you can give your own opinion of what was written. If you're unsure about what you read, it's wise to reread.

5. A typical news story is organized in an inverted pyramid. The lead comes first, followed by the most important details. Next are the less important details, ending with the least important details.

Multiple-choice Test
1. c   **2.** c   **3.** a   **4.** d   **5.** b

READING A BIOGRAPHY

Short-answer Test

1. A biography is the story of a real person's life. Fictional stories are not real.

2. Two goals of a biographer are to tell an interesting story and to create a "portrait," or impression, of the subject.

3. Sequence Notes can help you keep track of important events and when they occur.

4. Most biographies are organized in chronological order.

5. Outlining is a good strategy to use when rereading biographies. You can page through the book to review key events from the subject's life and add details to major topics in your Outline (such as "early years" or "young adulthood").

Multiple-choice Test
1. a   **2.** c   **3.** a   **4.** c   **5.** b

READING A MEMOIR

Short-answer Test

1. A memoir is autobiographical, a real story written by the person who lived it. A novel is fictional writing. Also, a memoir usually focuses on a part of the writer's life, and a novel is often a longer, more complete story.

2. *Answers may include three of the following:* reasons for the focus on a particular period in the writer's life, the writer's physical surroundings, actions and personalities of people the writer knew, the writer's work and major achievements, major problems and how the writer overcame them, and opinions and actions that reveal the writer's character and personality.

3. They are an organizer made up of two columns. They help you remember the main ideas of a piece of writing.

4. The two most common goals of a memoir writer are telling the story of part of his or her life in an interesting or dramatic way, and providing insight into the people, places, times, and events that influenced him or her.

5. Synthesizing involves pulling together different topics and looking at how they fit together as a whole. It is a useful strategy with memoirs because it helps you connect and relate key topics to get a complete "portrait" of a person, time, place, idea, or event.

Multiple-choice Test
1. d   **2.** c   **3.** a   **4.** b   **5.** d

FOCUS ON PERSUASIVE WRITING

Short-answer Test

1. *Answers may include three of the following:* to take action, spend money, accept an opinion, consider an idea, support a cause, and change your mind about something.

2. The three-step plan for reading persuasive writing helps you focus on the topic of the writing and what the writer is saying about that topic. Then you can decide for yourself what you think of what the writer is saying.

3. Reading critically helps you understand and evaluate the writer's assertion in a piece of persuasive writing. A critical reader can evaluate the quality of the argument.

4. The definition of *assertion* is a statement of belief that a writer explains and supports.

5. See page 233 for the names of eight common propaganda techniques and an example of each.

Multiple-choice Test
1. d **2.** d **3.** c **4.** a **5.** a

FOCUS ON SPEECHES

Short-answer Test

1. The purpose of an informative speech is to explain while the purpose of a persuasive speech is to persuade the audience to adopt the speaker's viewpoint.

2. Understanding the context of a speech means finding information about the time, place, and audience.

3. The three parts of a speech are the introduction, the body, and the conclusion.

4. *Answers may include three of the following:* facts and statistics, firsthand experiences or examples, opinions of experts, logical reasoning, comparisons and contrasts, research results, and appeals to emotion.

5. *Answers may include three of the following:* figurative language, repetition, parallelism, memorable sentences or phrases, and propaganda techniques.

Multiple-choice Test
1. a **2.** d **3.** c **4.** b **5.** c

ELEMENTS OF NONFICTION

Short-answer Test

1. An assertion is a claim, statement, or declaration that the writer supports with evidence or detail.

2. Deductive reasoning starts with a general statement, or assertion, and is followed with specific examples. Inductive reasoning starts with specific details and is followed with a broader, more general conclusion.

3. *Denotation* means a word's dictionary definition.

4. A rhetorical question is one asked for effect and to make a statement or point. No answer is expected. Students' examples will vary; one is provided on page 260 of the handbook.

5. Satire is often used to correct or change whatever the writer is targeting with the satire. Writers use satire to poke fun at human vices or weaknesses.

Multiple-choice Test
1. d   **2.** b   **3.** c   **4.** a   **5.** b

READING A SHORT STORY

Short-answer Test

1. Synthesizing involves looking at the parts of a piece of writing and pulling them together to help you answer questions about the writing.

2. A Fiction Organizer helps you focus on and make notes about six elements of a story: point of view, characters, setting, plot, theme, and style.

3. The traditional plot structure is exposition, rising action, climax, falling action, and resolution.

4. To connect a short story to your own life, think about any similarities between you and the characters in the story or between events in your life and those in the story. What do elements of the story remind you of in your own life? You can use a Making Connections Chart to relate to what you read.

5. Close reading is a good rereading strategy to use with short stories because it helps you answer any questions you may have after you read the story the first time. When you read more closely, you go more deeply into the details of story and its characters.

Multiple-choice Test
1. c   **2.** b   **3.** d   **4.** b   **5.** a

READING A NOVEL

Short-answer Test

1. *Answers may include four of the following:* point of view, characters, setting, plot, theme, and style.

2. *Answers may include two of the following:* Web, Fiction Organizer, Classification Notes, Character Map, Setting Chart, Summary Notes, Sequence Notes, Plot Diagram, Topic and Theme Organizer, and a Double-entry Journal.

3. The theme of a novel is the main idea that the author develops throughout the work. It is important because it is the author's "big message" to the reader.

4. *Answers may include three of the following:* sentence structure, tone, sensory details, word choice, dialogue, and figurative language.

5. Novels are longer than most other types of writing. You need a strategy so you don't get lost and so you understand what you're reading as you go through the novel.

Multiple-choice Test

1. b   **2.** c   **3.** d   **4.** d   **5.** b

FOCUS ON PLOT

Short-answer Test

1. The classic plot structure consists of the exposition, rising action, climax, falling action, and resolution of a story.

2. The beginning of most fiction pieces tells you the setting, characters, and source of conflict in the story.

3. The definition of *flashback* is a reference to an event or events that happened before the time of the story.

4. The definition of *subplot* is a story within the main story of a piece of fiction.

5. Understanding how a story's action unfolds (the plot) can help you understand how the author develops a point or lesson about life. You should focus on why certain events are included, differences between the rising action and the falling action, and how the climax relates to possible themes.

Multiple-choice Test

1. b   **2.** d   **3.** c   **4.** a   **5.** b

FOCUS ON SETTING

Short-answer Test

1. Clues that tell you when and where a story happens are usually found in the early pages of the story.

2. An immediate setting is the specific place and time in which part of a story takes place.

3. Mood is the feeling a story creates in you. Writers use the sensory details of a setting to create the mood of a story.

4. Using the strategy of close reading gives you an opportunity to take time and examine the specific details of the setting of a story.

5. Sketching a setting helps you see it more clearly and helps you see its significance to the story. Visualizing can spark your imagination and enhance your understanding.

Multiple-choice Test
1. d   **2.** c   **3.** a   **4.** b   **5.** c

FOCUS ON CHARACTERS

Short-answer Test

1. The protagonist is the main character, and the antagonist is the person or thing working against the main character.

2. A story's round characters are more developed, and more important, than flat characters.

3. Authors create characters by describing their physical appearance and personality; their speech, thoughts, feelings, actions, and desires; their interactions with other characters; their personal history or other background information; and by making direct comments about the character.

4. A dynamic character is one who changes and grows.

5. An Inference Chart is a good tool for keeping track of what characters reveal about themselves and for helping you interpret that information. In the left column you list details of what characters say and do. In the right column you note what you can conclude about them.

Multiple-choice Test
1. a   **2.** b   **3.** c   **4.** d   **5.** d

Reader's Handbook Test Book

FOCUS ON THEME

Short-answer Test

1. A theme consists of interwoven ideas that hold a story or novel together. The themes of a story are the larger ideas that comment on the story's subject. Some works have more than one theme.

2. The three steps for finding the theme in a literary work are identifying the "big ideas" or central topics, finding out what the characters do or say that relates to the central topics, and stating what the author says about life that relates to the central topics.

3. See the table at the bottom of page 346 for a list of common topics used for themes.

4. A Double-entry Journal helps you look at specific lines and parts of a literary work to see what they mean and how they relate to the topic and what a writer's message is.

5. The theme of a literary work is important because it is the "big idea" of the work, the writer's message about life that he or she wants to get across to the audience.

Multiple-choice Test

1. b   **2.** d   **3.** c   **4.** d   **5.** a

FOCUS ON DIALOGUE

Short-answer Test

1. Dialogue is the text in a story that characters say to each other.

2. Dialogue usually appears inside a set of quotation marks. Writers often begin a new paragraph each time a different character speaks and use speech tags to show who is talking.

3. Close reading is a good strategy to use when reading dialogue because it helps you to focus on who is talking and what they say. When you read closely, you think about what the characters' words reveal.

4. Dialogue allows a character to reveal clues about himself or herself, helping to develop the character for you. What words characters use and how they talk reveals a lot about individual personalities.

5. Characters often talk about what happened before the time of the story, explaining the background of any conflict.

Multiple-choice Test

1. c   **2.** b   **3.** a   **4.** c   **5.** d

FOCUS ON COMPARING AND CONTRASTING

Short-answer Test

1. Comparing focuses on how things are similar. Contrasting focuses on how they are different.

2. *Answers may include three of the following:* the characters and what they are like; when and where the story takes place; the plot; the themes; who tells the story; and any words, phrases, or ideas that are repeated.

3. A Two-novel Map offers you a chart for listing all the ways in which two works differ or are similar, categorized by literary element, such as characters and setting. The organizer has two columns, one for each work being compared.

4. A Venn Diagram is a good tool for comparing a single element of two works. It includes two circles, where you can write notes about how the element is used in each of the two works. The two circles intersect at a third circle, where you can write notes about how the two works are similar.

5. See the graphic on page 364 for the questions you can ask before writing a comparison and contrast paper.

Multiple-choice Test
1. b   **2.** d   **3.** a   **4.** a   **5.** a

ELEMENTS OF FICTION

Short-answer Test

1. The protagonist is the main character while the antagonist works against the main character.

2. Characterization is a technique used by authors to bring an imaginary person or creature to life by describing aspects of the character's appearance and personality; speech, thoughts, feelings, actions, and desires; interactions with other characters; and personal history or other background information.

3. *Answers may include three of the following:* person against person, person against society, person against nature, person against self, and person against fate.

4. Foreshadowing provides hints or clues early in a story that anticipate what is to come. Authors use foreshadowing to increase suspense, contribute to the mood, and make the ending seem believable.

5. The five parts of a classic plot are exposition, rising action, climax, falling action, and resolution.

Multiple-choice Test
1. b   **2.** a   **3.** d   **4.** c   **5.** a

READING A POEM

Short-answer Test

1. Each time you read a poem, you can focus on a different aspect. The *Reader's Handbook* recommends that you read a poem five times: once for enjoyment, once for meaning, once for structure and language, once for mood and tone, and finally once more for enjoyment.

2. In a close reading of a poem, you look at every word and every line of the poem, allowing you to focus on their meaning and your feelings. That makes close reading an excellent strategy to use with poems.

3. A paraphrase is restating someone else's words. When you paraphrase a poem, you translate its lines in your own words, making it sound like your own style.

4. A Double-entry Journal is another good connection tool because you use it to record your reactions to particular lines of a poem, allowing you to better connect to the poem.

5. A sonnet is a particular kind of lyric poem. It has 14 lines. Most sonnets have a set rhythm and regular rhyme scheme.

Multiple-choice Test

1. d   **2.** d   **3.** c   **4.** a   **5.** b

FOCUS ON LANGUAGE

Short-answer Test

1. *Tone* means the author's or speaker's attitude toward the subject of the poem or the reader.

2. *Denotation* means the word's dictionary definition. *Connotation* means the feeling suggested by or associated with a word.

3. Figurative language goes beyond the literal meanings of words. Examples include similes, metaphors, and symbols.

4. Poets use imagery to startle you or to stimulate your senses.

5. Close reading of a poem helps you concentrate on every word and every line of the poem, allowing you to focus on meaning, figurative language, repetition, tone, mood, and imagery.

Multiple-choice Test

1. c   **2.** b   **3.** a   **4.** d   **5.** b

FOCUS ON MEANING

Short-answer Test

1. The subject of a poem is the topic. The meaning is the poet's attitude toward the topic, or the message of the poem.

2. A word has both a dictionary meaning (denotation) and an emotional impact on a reader (connotation). Recognizing both denotations and connotations of particular words in a poem can help you more easily decipher a poet's message.

3. Close reading of a poem helps you concentrate on every word and every line of the poem, allowing you to focus on meaning. When you paraphrase a poem, you restate its lines in your own words. That helps you understand what the lines mean.

4. A Double-entry Journal helps you record your reactions to particular lines of a poem, allowing you to better connect to the poem.

5. Your own feelings about a poem can provide clues to its meaning. Support your ideas and explain your reactions with specific words or phrases from the poem.

Multiple-choice Test
1. a   **2.** a   **3.** c   **4.** a   **5.** d

FOCUS ON SOUND AND STRUCTURE

Short-answer Test

1. Structure refers to a poem's organization or how it looks on the page—including stanza divisions and line length.

2. Close reading is a good strategy to use when focusing on the sound and structure of a poem because it slows you down as you read and allows you to focus on specific details of organization, rhyme, and rhythm.

3. *Alliteration* is the repetition of sounds at the beginnings of words.

4. *Assonance* refers to the repetition of vowel sounds in accented syllables that are close together.

5. The rhythm of a poem is its beat, the pattern of stressed and unstressed syllables in a poem.

Multiple-choice Test
1. b   **2.** d   **3.** a   **4.** b   **5.** c

ELEMENTS OF POETRY

Short-answer Test

1. Onomatopoeia is the use of words that imitate the sounds they describe, such as "whoosh."

2. A metaphor is a direct comparison of two unlike things and does not use the words *like* or *as*. A simile compares two unlike things using *like* or *as*.

3. Tone is the attitude the writer or speaker takes toward the audience, the subject, or a character.

4. Personification is a figure of speech in which poets give an animal, object, or idea, human qualities.

5. Hyperbole is exaggeration, the obvious stretching of the truth to emphasize strong feeling or to create humor.

Multiple-choice Test

1. c   **2.** b   **3.** a   **4.** b   **5.** d

READING A PLAY

Short-answer Test

1. First, plays are made up mostly of dialogue and stage directions, while novels and stories are made up of dialogue and narration. Second, plays are divided into acts and scenes, not chapters.

2. When you summarize a play, you retell the main events or ideas in your own words. This helps you keep track of setting, characters, the sequence of events, and themes, and helps you better understand the play's meaning.

3. A play is usually organized into two or three acts, with two or three scenes in each act.

4. A Plot Diagram is a visual representation of the five parts of a classic plot: exposition, rising action, climax, falling action, and resolution. As you write in the play's events in each part of the organizer, you can better analyze the play's action.

5. Plays are created to be seen and heard, so visualizing and thinking aloud is a good strategy to use in analyzing a play's story and dialogue. You can reread parts of the play and use sketches or Think Alouds to help you understand and review what's important.

Multiple-choice Test

1. b   **2.** c   **3.** d   **4.** b   **5.** a

FOCUS ON LANGUAGE

Short-answer Test

1. Three elements that can help you understand the language of a play are key lines and speeches, stage directions, and dialogue.

2. Stage directions tell the actors and director how to perform the play, how to arrange the stage, and how the actors should move and talk.

3. *Answers may include two of the following:* establishes character, advances the plot, and reveals the theme(s).

4. An Inference Chart helps you keep a record of your conclusions about characters.

5. A Paraphrase Chart can help you remember key passages of a play, because you restate those passages in your own words.

Multiple-choice Test

1. a   **2.** c   **3.** d   **4.** b   **5.** d

FOCUS ON THEME

Short-answer Test

1. The theme of a play is the playwright's message to the audience about the topic of the play.

2. The plan for understanding theme in the handbook has three steps: finding the major ideas or general topics of the play, noticing what the characters do and say that relates to the general topics, and coming up with a statement of the playwright's point or message about these topics.

3. A Topic and Theme Organizer helps you keep track of the "big ideas" of a play and your thoughts about those ideas. You can then come up with a statement of the theme based on your notes in this organizer. Filling our the organizer requires you to find details in the text to support theme statements.

4. The topic is the subject, or "big idea," of the play. The theme is the playwright's message about that topic.

5. A Main Idea Organizer helps you check out a possible theme by asking you to find at least three supporting details in the play for that theme.

Multiple-choice Test

1. a   **2.** c   **3.** d   **4.** b   **5.** d

FOCUS ON SHAKESPEARE

Short-answer Test

1. Shakespeare's plays are challenging because the plays are longer, usually divided into five acts, and the language and style can be difficult to understand.

2. To read a Shakespearean play, first read the entire play for sense. Second, reread key scenes, looking for specifics.

3. Summary Notes can help you keep track of the characters and the plot in a Shakespearean play. As you read, write down the key events in each scene in each act.

4. Three tips for understanding Shakespeare are listed and explained in the table on page 493 of the handbook.

5. Love and revenge are two common topics in Shakespeare's plays.

Multiple-choice Test

1. c   **2.** d   **3.** b   **4.** a   **5.** b

ELEMENTS OF DRAMA

Short-answer Test

1. Plays are often divided into two or three acts, each of which usually contains two or three scenes.

2. The chorus often describes and comments on the main action of the play, offering additional explanation to the audience.

3. Stage directions are a playwright's instructions to the actors and director that tell how to stage and perform a play.

4. *Aside* refers to a remark NOT intended to be heard by other characters. Monologue means a speech by a character who is alone on stage or apart from other characters.

5. While a play's plot is the central action of the play, the subplot is a less important story that takes place alongside the main plot.

Multiple-choice Test

1. b   **2.** c   **3.** d   **4.** c   **5.** a

READING A WEBSITE

Short-answer Test

1. Before reading a website, you should set a purpose for reading. Ask yourself, "What is it I hope to find on this site?"

2. *Answers may include three of the following:* the name and overall appearance of the site, the main menu or table of contents, the source or sponsor, any description of what it contains, any images or graphics that create a feeling, and the purpose of the site.

3. When you read critically, you read slowly, gathering information and taking the time to evaluate that information. That is crucial to determining if a website is reliable.

4. Skimming is a strategy that involves looking over material quickly and not reading word for word. One tip is looking for general ideas, paying attention to such things as the source of the site, headings, and any repeated words. A second tip is not to read everything. Skip information that doesn't meet your needs or seems to be inaccurate or inappropriate.

5. A Website Profiler helps you organize your notes and thoughts about a site and evaluate its reliability. You can then keep the Website Profiler in a safe place and return to it if you want to revisit the site.

Multiple-choice Test

1. c   **2.** c   **3.** d   **4.** d   **5.** b

ELEMENTS OF THE INTERNET

Short-answer Test

1. A search engine is a tool for finding information on the Internet. You type in the terms you want to search for, and the search engine then lists the addresses of sites where those terms appear.

2. The header of an email usually includes the subject of the email, the date and time it was sent, the sender's email address, and the address of the person to whom it is being sent.

3. A newsgroup is an online discussion area where people with a specific interest post messages.

4. The World Wide Web is a system of computers around the world that are joined and able to share files.

5. Common elements of websites include a browser, features (such as pop-up menus, boxes to enter search terms, arrows and buttons, and so on), links, plug-in applications, and the URL.

Multiple-choice Test

1. b   **2.** a   **3.** a   **4.** c   **5.** d

READING A GRAPHIC

Short-answer Test

1. *Answers may include three of the following:* the title or heading; any captions or background text; any labels and column and row headings; any colors, patterns, icons, or other symbols; any keys or legends; the scale or unit of measurement; and the source of both the graphic and its data.

2. The plan for reading a graphic includes these five steps: scanning the graphic to develop an overall impression of its content and possible meaning; reading all of the text, including captions; telling in your own words what the graphic shows; thinking about the quality, meaning, and purpose of the information; and making a connection with the graphic.

3. When you paraphrase a graphic, you put the information into your own words, which helps you better understand what the graphic shows.

4. A Critical Reading Chart is a good tool for reading graphics because it helps you question what you find in a graphic, organize your thoughts, and evaluate your findings.

5. The bottom rule, or line, of a graphic is its horizontal axis. The rule on the left side is the vertical axis. Sometimes the rules are missing, but there is text showing the axes on the left and bottom instead. The legend, or key, explains the different colors, abbreviations, symbols, shapes, icons, or line patterns in a graphic.

Multiple-choice Test
1. b   **2.** a   **3.** d   **4.** c   **5.** c

ELEMENTS OF GRAPHICS

Short-answer Test

1. A cartoon is a drawing that makes humorous but meaningful comments about life and society.

2. A flow chart is a visual picture that shows the order of operations used to create a product, make a decision, or complete a process.

3. The kinds of maps and what they show are listed in the table on page 562 of the handbook.

4. A pie chart, usually shown in the form of a circle, shows parts that make up a whole.

5. A timeline shows a series of events organized in chronological, or time, order.

Multiple-choice Test
1. b   **2.** a   **3.** d   **4.** c   **5.** c

READING A DRIVER'S HANDBOOK

Short-answer Test

1. *Answers may include any of the following:* the table of contents; any headings; any words in large type, boldface type, or all capital letters; any numbered or bulleted lists; and any graphic elements, such as illustrations and diagrams.

2. Skimming is a good strategy because when you skim, you read quickly, looking for specific information and trying to get a general sense of the content.

3. Summary Notes help you remember what you've read. Your notes can be as detailed as you like, and you can always return to reread what you've written on this organizer.

4. You use two columns. On the left, list key words or topics. On the right, note important information.

5. After you've finished reading, ask yourself if you've accomplished your purpose and whether anything confused you.

Multiple-choice Test

1. c   **2.** c   **3.** b   **4.** a   **5.** b

FOCUS ON READING INSTRUCTIONS

Short-answer Test

1. To set a purpose for reading instructions, preview the instructions. Look at the title and headings, the steps in the process, any diagrams or graphics, any key words in boldface or capital letters, and any bulleted lists. Then you will have a better idea of what you want to get out of the reading.

2. Close reading is a good strategy to use when reading instructions because it makes you slow down and read word for word, sentence by sentence, or line by line.

3. *Answers may include two of the following:* highlighting or marking words and phrases, think aloud about the steps, reread for understanding, read one step at a time, reading any diagrams, and asking yourself questions as you read.

4. Thinking aloud helps you put the directions in your own words, making them easier to understand and remember.

5. If you can't accomplish what you need to do after following the instructions the first time, you can either ask a friend to read the instructions and help you or you can go back through the directions and check off each step as you go.

Multiple-choice Test

1. c   **2.** c   **3.** b   **4.** a   **5.** d

FOCUS ON READING FOR WORK

Short-answer Test

1. The four steps for understanding workplace reading are identifying the reason you're reading, understanding the way the writing is organized, finding what you need to know, and applying the information to your own life to help you remember it.

2. To set a purpose for reading work-related materials, you should think about what you already know about the topic. Then, think about what you want to look for in the reading.

3. Skimming is a good strategy to use when reading work-related materials because when you skim, you look quickly at the material, watching for headings, boldface type, bulleted lists, and any other elements that stand out. You then slow down to focus on those items, looking for key words.

4. *Answers may include one of the following:* reading titles or headings, highlighting important information and key words, and connecting the information to yourself.

5. If you can't find the information you need, reread more slowly and look at headings, boldface type, and words that start with capital letters in order to find key information. Another strategy is to ask a friend for help.

Multiple-choice Test
1. b   **2.** b   **3.** d   **4.** c   **5.** d

READING TESTS AND TEST QUESTIONS

Short-answer Test

1. The steps for answering test questions are reading the passage or test items, reading the question and looking for key words, and skimming the passage for key words and the answers.

2. Skimming is a good strategy to use on tests because when you skim, you look quickly at the material, watching for key words that indicate the answers to specific questions.

3. The three basic types of test questions are factual recall questions, critical thinking questions, and essay questions.

4. A Main Idea Organizer is a good tool to use for answering essay questions because it helps you organize your writing before you get started.

5. After a test is over, talk to a classmate about the questions you had trouble with to see if the other student can give you any insight you can use on a future test. You should also test yourself by asking yourself about how well prepared you were and what you might do differently for your next test.

Multiple-choice Test
1. d   **2.** d   **3.** a   **4.** a   **5.** b

FOCUS ON ENGLISH TESTS

Short-answer Test

1. *Answers may include two of the following:* making note cards, taking a practice test, building your vocabulary, and learning key grammar and punctuation rules.

2. Tips for improving your vocabulary include looking up words you don't know when you find them in stories and books you read, placing these new words in a vocabulary notebook or on file cards, and working to remember these new words.

3. Word analogies test your knowledge of word relationships in pairs of words.

4. Preview an English test by looking at the kinds of questions on the test. You should answer the easiest questions first, and skim for key words. Use reading strategies such as thinking aloud to help you answer questions calling for inferences.

5. English tests usually contain reading passage questions; grammar, usage, and mechanics questions; and vocabulary questions.

Multiple-choice Test
1. b   **2.** a   **3.** a   **4.** c   **5.** b

FOCUS ON WRITING TESTS

Short-answer Test

1. The basic areas usually covered on a writing test are correcting sentence errors, improving sentences and paragraphs, and responding to essay questions in timed writings.

2. *Answers may include two of the following:* preparing by reviewing the basics, taking a practice test, talking to others, or making a plan for answering essay questions; previewing the test to see what types of questions are on it; reading the directions carefully; reading the possible answers, reading the writing prompt; and using your writing plan.

3. Your essay should have a topic sentence, support for the topic sentence, and a conclusion.

4. The three common kinds of writing prompts are personal, social, and academic.

5. A Main Idea Organizer works well to help you organize your thoughts and supporting details.

Multiple-choice Test
1. a   **2.** d   **3.** a   **4.** a   **5.** d

FOCUS ON STANDARDIZED TESTS

Short-answer Test

1. *Answers may include two of the following:* visiting the test website, taking a practice test, preparing yourself mentally and physically, and trying to relax.

2. Previewing a test allows you to find the easiest questions so you can go back and answer those first and then plan to allow extra time for more challenging questions.

3. Thinking aloud is a strategy that helps you sort out your thoughts as you answer questions.

4. *Answers may include two of the following:* eliminating those answers that "sound wrong" to you, those that are only partially true, those that don't "fit" with an answer you substitute, and those that don't have the information called for in the question.

5. Check your work and erase stray marks on the answer sheet. If you won't be penalized for guessing, make sure that every question has an answer.

Multiple-choice Test
1. d   **2.** c   **3.** a   **4.** d   **5.** b

FOCUS ON HISTORY TESTS

Short-answer Test

1. Possible answers include rereading the text material you'll be tested on, reviewing your class notes and study guides, creating a top ten list, and practicing how to read graphics.

2. To preview a history test, read the directions for special instructions and for time limits. Then glance at other pages of the test, taking note of questions with graphics, which will need extra time.

3. A "top ten list" is a list you make of the ten most important topics you need to study for a test.

4. If you're unsure of the answer to a question on a history test, start by crossing out the answers that you know are wrong. Beware of partially true answers, and talk yourself through other possible answers

5. When you come to a graphic on a history test, pause and look at the entire graphic. Consider its larger message. Make notes if you can about the "big picture."

Multiple-choice Test
1. b   **2.** c   **3.** d   **4.** a   **5.** d

FOCUS ON MATH TESTS

Short-answer Test

1. To prepare for a math test, you should review old homework assignments, quizzes, and tests, reworking practice problems. Then skim your math text, looking at graphics and thinking through example problems. Last, memorize key terms, rules, and formulas.

2. When you preview, find out what kind of questions to expect. Put a star by the ones that you think will be the easiest.

3. Visualizing makes a math problem clearer and helps you organize your work.

4. When you plug an answer choice into an equation, you can solve the equation and see which multiple-choice possibility is correct.

5. After finishing a test, go back and check your work, especially those problems that you found most difficult to answer. If there's no penalty for guessing, be sure you have answered every question.

Multiple-choice Test
1. b   **2.** d   **3.** a   **4.** b   **5.** c

FOCUS ON SCIENCE TESTS

Short-answer Test

1. When you come across a new term in your science text, look it up in the text's glossary or a dictionary. Write the definition in your science notebook.

2. When you preview, skim the directions. Then quickly read a few questions, and mark the easy ones to answer first. Glance at any charts, graphs, or diagrams.

3. Visualizing and thinking aloud is a good strategy for answering questions on science tests.

4. The three steps for answering a reasoning question are reading the data and being sure what you need to find out, coming up with a hypothesis, and reading the possible answers.

5. Making an educated guess involves eliminating all but two answer choices for a question, rereading the question to look for clues, and then thinking through each remaining choice before selecting the best answer.

Multiple-choice Test
1. a   **2.** c   **3.** d   **4.** c   **5.** d

IMPROVING VOCABULARY

Short-answer Test

1. *Answers may include three of the following:* keeping a vocabulary journal, looking up words, pronouncing words, making Study or Note Cards, learning words every day, using new words, and creating Concept Maps.

2. *Answers may include three of the following:* definitions or synonyms, concrete examples, contrast clues, description clues, words or phrases that modify, conjunctions showing relationships, and unstated or implied meanings of words.

3. A word root is the part of a word that carries its meaning. Examples will vary. See the list on pages 762–765.

4. A suffix is added at the end of a word root. A prefix is added in front of a word root.

5. *Analogy* means an expression that shows how two things are similar. Examples will vary, and could include the following: happy : sad :: large : small (antonyms) and antenna : phone :: keypad : microwave (whole and part).

Multiple-choice Test

1. c **2.** a **3.** d **4.** a **5.** d

DOING RESEARCH

Short-answer Test

1. The reading process includes the same steps as the research process. You set a purpose, preview (when you gather your materials for research), plan, read with a purpose, connect, pause and reflect, reread, and remember (when you use a strategy such as note-taking to help you keep track of the information you've gathered).

2. A primary source is an original source, such as a diary or memoir. A secondary source is one that contains information other people have gathered and interpreted. The chart on page 696 of the handbook gives examples of secondary sources and tells where you can find them, such as in libraries and on the Internet.

3. The Source Evaluator is an excellent reading tool to use in evaluating a source. It gives you a place to organize information about the source itself and a place for you to write your thoughts about the source.

4. You must be careful to use quotation marks and ellipses when recording exact passages from sources to be accurate, and avoid plagiarism, or passing off someone else's work as your own.

5. Informal documentation refers to naming a source or sources within the body of your presentation or report. No further referencing is needed. Formal documentation refers to the use of parenthetical references and list of sources to provide complete publication about the material you use.

Multiple-choice Test

1. a **2.** d **3.** d **4.** c **5.** c